D1712445

Praise for *The Honeymoon of Your Dreams*

The Honeymoon of Your Dreams is a book that will help couples get started from day one with developing the right skills for living together. The positive financial results of a marriage built on a proper foundation will impact not only the marriage, but future generations as well. This book is bound to have a very long life.

Ron Blue
President, Christian Financial Professionals Network
Author, *Master Your Money*

This is some of the most practical, sensible, wise and God-honoring advice I have ever read on this subject. I read everything Dr. Walt Larimore writes and, combined with Dr. Susan Crockett, they have created what will be a "classic" on this subject. When my three daughters get married, I will hand them this book.

Jim Burns, Ph.D.
President, HomeWord
Author, *Creating an Intimate Marriage*

This is a long-overdue book. As a seminary professor, I want to get this into the hands of my students for them to give copies to all of the couples they counsel.

Lyle W. Dorsett
Billy Graham Professor of Evangelism
Beeson Divinity School at Samford University
Birmingham, Alabama

This book is a delightful gem, full of practical wisdom and sound medical suggestions to start a God-honoring marriage on the proper foundation. Perfect for couples planning to marry as well as a marvelous resource for pastors, counselors and family members who love them! Even the appendices, websites listed and the bibliography are loaded with pearls.

William R. Cutrer, MD
Gheens Professor of Christian Ministry
The Southern Baptist Theological Seminary

The Honeymoon of Your Dreams is medically reliable, biblically sound advice that should be packaged with every engagement ring. It will be the first book I give when my two unmarried children decide to marry. It should be subtitled, "A Marriage Insurance Policy."

David Stevens, MD, MA
Executive Director, Christian Medical and Dental Associations
Bristol, Tennessee

As a professional Christian psychiatrist, I found myself blown away with the new insights in *The Honeymoon of Your Dreams*. The book not only gave excellent medical, theological and psychological advice for the honeymoon period but also excellent advice on premarital counseling, communications and a host of other helpful areas of marital adjustments. I highly recommend this book not only for the bride and groom but also for the parents of the bride and groom and even for professional therapists like myself.

Paul Meier, MD
Author of over 70 books
Founder of the national chain of Meier Clinics
Dallas, Texas

The Honeymoon of Your Dreams is a great book that fills a void in the library of every pastor and Christian counselor. It is easy to read and filled with useful information. I learned things I wished I had known 35 years ago.

Ed Dawson, MS
Clinical Psychologist
Lexington, North Carolina

I wish to express my enthusiastic endorsement of this writing as scripturally and spiritually rock-solid. I only regret that my wife, Laura, and I were not able to draw on the great insights and suggestions set forth in this book when we were married. I plan on sharing this information with my two children when the time is right.

Rick Fisher
Elder Council
Little Log Church
Palmer Lake, Colorado

Thanks to Walt and Sue for such a practical, scriptural, well-written and well-designed resource. This book masterfully addresses (and closes) the biggest hole in premarital counseling in the North American Church. It is a resource I can confidently recommend to patients and friends alike.

Burritt W. Hess, MD
Family Physician
Gatesville, Texas

What a wonderful resource! Walt Larimore and Susan Crockett have written an unflinchingly honest and biblically accurate handbook for honeymooners. I already have patients to whom I can't wait to give this book.

Julian T. Hsu, MD
Family Physician
Denver, Colorado

I highly recommend this book for all engaged couples. Drs. Crockett and Larimore are on to something with the importance they place on the honeymoon as a significant launching pad for marriage.

Dr. Layne Lebo
Senior Pastor
Mechanicsburg Brethren in Christ Church
Mechanicsburg, Pennsylvania

THE
HONEYMOON
of Your Dreams

Walt Larimore, MD
Susan Crockett, MD

Regal

From Gospel Light
Ventura, California, U.S.A.

Published by Regal Books
From Gospel Light
Ventura, California, U.S.A.
Printed in the U.S.A.

Library of Congress Cataloging-in-Publication Data
Larimore, Walter L.
    The honeymoon of your dreams / Walt Larimore, Susan Crockett.
        p. cm.
    Includes bibliographical references and indexes.
    ISBN 0-8307-4313-8 (hard cover) — ISBN 0-8307-4393-6 (international trade paper)
    1. Honeymoons. 2. Sex—Religious aspects—Christianity. 3. Marriage—Religious aspects—Christianity.
I. Crockett, Susan. II. Title.
    BV835.L353 2007
    248.8'44—dc22   2006033138

Note: This book contains advice and information relating to your health. It is designed for your personal knowledge and to help you be a more informed consumer of medical and health services. It is not intended to be exhaustive or to replace medical advice from your personal physician and should be used to supplement rather than replace regular care by a physician. Readers are encouraged to consult their personal physician with any specific questions or concerns. Under no circumstances should you take or use any medication of any kind without first checking with your physician. All efforts have been made to ensure the accuracy of the information contained within this book as of the date published. The authors and the publisher expressly disclaim responsibility for any adverse effects resulting from the application of the information contained herein. While all of the stories told in this book are true to life, names have been changed in most instances in order to preserve the privacy of those involved.

*This book is lovingly dedicated to
Barb Larimore and Dale Crockett,
who first showed us through their love
the divine design for marriage—
that of a lifelong honeymoon.*

CONTENTS

Part Four

INTRODUCTION

*For this reason a man will leave his father and mother and be united
to his wife, and they will become one flesh.*

GENESIS 2:24

We've got some great news concerning *your* honeymoon. The divine design is that you and your spouse-to-be experience great enjoyment loving each other! You've been created with this capacity, and the marital relationship is the place to express it! After all, your marriage and honeymoon are the foundation for the first and most important of all divinely prescribed institutions: the family.

Whether you made a commitment in the past to remain a virgin until your wedding night or you have already had sexual experiences, we've written this book to give you practical, medically reliable, trustworthy and biblically sound advice regarding your honeymoon and marriage.

The book is divided into four parts:

Part 1: Planning and Preparation for the Honeymoon
(chapters 1–7)
Part 2: Special Sections for the Bride's Eyes and the Groom's
Eyes Only (chapters 8–9)
Part 3: The First 7 Days—Daily Reflections for the
Honeymoon (chapter 10)
Part 4: Helpful Appendices

Please resist the temptation to skip straight to the chapters for the bride's and the groom's eyes only! We encourage you to read the whole book. The planning and preparation chapters are the foundation to having the honeymoon of a lifetime, and you'll be cutting yourself short by skipping through and grabbing out bits and pieces.

In Part 1, we'll start by sharing some of the biblical foundations and principles of marriage. Even if you are not one of those couples for whom religion is a core experience, we believe that the proven wisdom of the Bible, combined with the best of science, is applicable to all men and women facing marriage. After all, there's a reason that most people believe the Bible is not just a good book but *the* Good Book. Think of it as a user's manual for your life.

We'll explore the divine design for your honeymoon and your marriage and subsequent sexual relationship (you may be quite surprised to find that the Bible actually has quite a lot to say about sex!).

We'll continue with chapters about preparing spiritually for physical intimacy and discuss virginity, secondary virginity and the significance of sexual purity before and during your marriage—even if you're currently sexually active.

We will also briefly address medical and travel concerns and will include a chapter on suggestions about what to pack for your honeymoon. The material in Part 1 is intended to be read as far in advance of your wedding as possible; we recommend that you and your fiancé read Part 1 together.

Part 2 is a special section containing two chapters: "For the Bride's Eyes Only" and "For the Groom's Eyes Only." These two unique chapters contain sexually intimate material and advice straight from Dr. Sue to the bride and from Dr. Walt to the groom.

"For the Bride's Eyes Only" contains practical information that a soon-to-be bride's physician should discuss with her but probably won't. This counsel from Dr. Sue and other married women is distilled from generations of practical woman-to-woman wisdom compiled from our exclusive honeymoon survey. The chapter includes instructions that we don't think you'll find anywhere else for making your own Honeymoon Kit. Likewise, the groom's chapter contains a man-to-man discussion from Dr. Walt that serves as a unique and vital message for the prospective groom.

These chapters contain frank, practical and biblical advice for the honeymoon. Because of the sexually explicit nature of these chapters and the possibility for increasing sexual temptation prior to your wedding, we recommend that you do not read these chapters until one to two weeks before your honeymoon.

Spiritual intimacy is such a critical part of marriage that we have devoted Part 3 solely to that subject. This section contains seven daily reflections for your first week of marriage. This special section is designed to help you, as a newlywed couple, develop the important habit of spending spiritually intimate time together. You'll find a new topic for each day, with a short devotional written especially for your first week as a new family. Be sure to bring this book with you on the honeymoon, as Part 3 is to be saved for the honeymoon itself.

Part 4 includes several appendices designed to help you prepare for and have the honeymoon of your dreams—the honeymoon of a lifetime. There's a brief version of the instructions for the Honeymoon Kit that you can copy for easy reference while on your honeymoon. This material includes a shopping/packing list for the kit contents. There's also a six-month calendar countdown for honeymoon preparation.

We believe that our perspective as physicians and long-time premarital counselors, as well as our viewpoint as students of the Bible, will give you extraordinary insight into one of the most critical events of your life—your first night and first week as husband and wife. Walt is a family physician with more than 20 years of clinical experience, and Sue is an obstetrician/gynecologist who graduated from medical school in the early 1990s. The combination of our voices—male and female, and from different medical specialties and different decades of training—weaves together a comfortable, warm quilt in the form of a well-balanced book packed full of meaningful, useful information for planning your honeymoon.

For the sake of clarity, the majority of this book is written using Walt's voice, although the chapter "For the Bride's Eyes Only" is written primarily in Sue's voice, speaking woman-to-woman to the prospective bride.

We invite you to take your time as you read each section, reflecting on the stories of those who have taken this special journey before you, so that you and your soul mate can begin to not only plan a wedding but also prepare your heart for marriage. The two of you, just as all those who have traveled this road before you, will have your own story to tell on the other side of your honeymoon.

We pray that this book will help you and your fiancé lay a foundation for successfully launching your married life, and that you will find great joy together in your honeymoon journey. And we hope that the wisdom you apply, and the knowledge you gain, will allow you to share your story and advice with those who follow you.

Walt Larimore, MD
Monument, Colorado
Susan Crockett, MD
San Antonio, Texas
October 2006

Part One

Chapter One

REDEFINING THE HONEYMOON

And now these three remain: faith, hope and love.
But the greatest of these is love.

1 CORINTHIANS 13:13

So, how are your wedding plans coming along?"
If you're a prospective bride, it's likely that you will hear this phrase countless times before your wedding. Everyone wants to hear about your gown, your veil, the reception, the cake, the flowers, the invitations and all the numerous details of preparation that go into the planning of your wedding. And you are delighted to talk about these things.

Did you know that there is another event other than your wedding ceremony and reception that critically needs your attention and planning? Few engaged couples, however, know how to proceed with plans for this life-altering event called the honeymoon. What follows is the story of a young couple who sadly experienced this reality.

Karen's Story

Karen was one of those perfect brides. She was model beautiful, smart and wealthy and had a very handsome fiancé. Karen and Tom were a gorgeous couple. Karen had the perfect dress, the most expensive reception, the most exclusive guests and 10 bridesmaids and groomsmen to flank her wedding party. Every detail was scheduled and prepared for down to the smallest nuance—and it was a fabulous wedding and reception. From the outside, it appeared to be an event to remember for a lifetime.

Karen and Tom's hundreds of guests saw them off after the reception. How happy everyone was for them! And the tired but happy couple was excited to spend their first night together as husband and wife and depart on their honeymoon. They were scheduled to leave on a plane early the next morning for a fantastic, dreamy European honeymoon. What a fairy tale come true! Or so they thought.

They returned from their honeymoon a week later with their fairytale bubble shattered. It had been a nightmare of a honeymoon.

Karen sobbed as she confided to her girlfriends the events of the previous week, starting with the wedding night. Karen and Tom had not left the reception until close to midnight, and she had eaten little food all day. Most of her time at the reception had been spent socializing with many of the more than 500 guests. The newlyweds arrived at their hotel that night exhausted and hungry.

Karen had given in to Tom's pressure to have sex during their engagement, and she still harbored some bitterness about the fact that she had given away her virginity on a night that was not her wedding night. She didn't really care if *it* didn't happen this night; there was always tomorrow to consummate their marriage. They both crashed sound asleep in each others' arms.

The next day, their travel alarm did not go off. They jumped out of bed with no time for romance and hurriedly showered, packed up, ran to the airport, were delayed by the security lines and just about missed their international flight.

After several flight connections (including another one they very nearly missed) and a *long* day of travel, they finally arrived at their destination jet-lagged and even more exhausted than the night before. All Karen could think about was getting to their nice, plush hotel room, their comfy, plush bed, and crashing. But all Tom could think of was having sex with his new bride, again and again, in their sumptuous and swanky hotel room.

However, neither the room nor the bed was lush or lavish. Those of you with travel experience will understand what happened. What is considered a four-star hotel in the United States does not necessarily translate to the same standard overseas.

The accommodations were clean but small and cramped, with painted pipes overhead. And they had an awfully uncomfortable—even lumpy—mattress. The bride, the princess, the perfectionist was beyond unhappy. But at least they had each other, right? And sex!

Well, that actually was great, despite the lumpy bed—although Karen was surprised at how she found herself resenting even more the fact that Tom could not have waited for sex until the honeymoon.

Then, to make things worse, Karen came down with a bad bladder infection, what we doctors call a rip-roaring case of honeymoon cystitis, the very next day—fever, pain and a honey-you-can-forget-about-any-more-fun-down-there-for-a-while kind of cystitis.

Ever try finding medical care in a foreign country? It took Karen and Tom most of the next day and a big chunk of their extra honeymoon money to get her the medical treatment she needed.

To make a rapidly souring situation even worse, several lingering relational issues came up, leading to several loud and long arguments—the last one resulting in Karen dissolving in tears and Tom storming out of the hotel. Karen wished they had taken a friend's advice to get some premarital counseling. She was stunned at the completely unexpected depression, loneliness and homesickness that invaded her soul. When she called her mom and talked for more than 30 minutes, Tom blew a gasket and again left her alone, which only worsened her misery.

By then, they had both had it. All they could think of was getting home. Which they did—two days earlier than scheduled—and for a significant add-on cost for changing airline tickets.

Karen and Tom can't forget about their honeymoon. It's a nightmare that continues to haunt them both. It still affects Tom's feelings for Karen. He actually thought about suggesting they go to counseling, but he has decided to bury the whole thing emotionally—except he can't do that.

Unfortunately, this couple did not see that their terrible honeymoon experience had the potential to eventually lead to a wrecked marriage.

Poor Karen—she had the perfect wedding and the perfect husband. Why did she have a honeymoon that went all wrong? Was this any way to start a marriage? What could have been done to prevent this nightmare from happening?

Wrong Ideas About Honeymoons!

Although there is help and advice for the wedding and reception plans, much less frequently will anyone ask about your honeymoon preparation and plans—and if they do, the questions are usually superficial, such as, "Where are you going on your trip?" "How long will you be gone?" "Where will you be staying?" Hardly ever will you be asked questions about the details of your preparation for the first week of the rest of your life together as husband and wife.

Why is this? Is it because it's too intimate? Too personal? Too much information?

Perhaps these are some of the reasons, but we suspect there are two far more important reasons: (1) Most men and women simply do not understand how critical their honeymoon is to the health of their marriage; and (2) Most married couples simply do not plan the life-changing event upon which they will embark—their honeymoon.

Not only do we not ask about the honeymoon, but we also aren't taught about it. Parents typically are caught up in the wedding ceremony. Pastors, priests and rabbis usually concentrate on compatibility issues and conflict-resolution skills. Certainly, most of our friends don't feel equipped to teach us *anything* concerning matrimony. Who feels equipped to teach while either looking for their own future mate or trying to maintain their own marriage?

Simply put, our society in general, and the Church in particular, places more emphasis on planning the wedding than planning the honeymoon—an experience that occupies the first and most critical week of virtually all marriages.

Check it out for yourself. Look at the $72 billion wedding industry. Peruse the hundreds of wedding magazines, guides and books. Look at the content of these publications: You will find scads of information and advice on all the trappings of a fairy-tale ceremony but pitifully little guidance concerning your honeymoon—the beginning of your married life together. Most women (or their mothers) heading toward a wedding have shelves filled with several resources of marketing information for the things and events that should surround the planning of the wedding ceremony—but almost nothing on preparing for the rest of their life.

And if there's *any* information to be found on the honeymoon, it typically only discusses where to go, how to get there and what you should expect or do sexually. Go to a book site on the Internet, like www.amazon.com or www.barnesandnoble.com, and search using the word "honeymoon." Besides the novels, travel guides, sex guides and journals, there's nothing to help *you* prepare for this foundational week of your marriage and life together with your soul mate.

Our culture, churches and communities—not to mention our families, friends and faith communities—have abandoned the traditional practices of our ancestors of passing down wisdom from grandmother, aunt or mother to the prospective bride—or from grandfather, uncle or father to the prospective groom. Unfortunately, it seems that this brand of wisdom has been buried with past generations.

As a result, what we have found in our medical practices, after more than 35 collective years of practicing medicine, is that there are now more and more engaged couples turning to us, as their physicians, for answers to their most intimate questions and concerns about the honeymoon.

Although this happened less commonly when we were new in our practices, it seems to us that increasingly couples intuitively understand that their honeymoon is not just another vacation. It's the beginning of a new life with their soul mate—and like a foot race, the start will dramatically determine the finish.

Not only do most men and women have medical and sexual concerns about their honeymoon, but even more important, they express real, heartfelt questions about preparing for the emotional, relational and spiritual changes that they hope will occur when two souls take the most holy, until-death-do-us-part vow of their lifetime—the sacred promises of matrimony.

These conversations require trust and openness. They are the kinds of conversations once reserved only for parents, close relatives and friends or the parish priest, the local pastor or rabbi. However, because most modern family members and pastoral professionals simply don't know where to start, we doctors are hearing these questions in our practices. Like most physicians, we treasure our relationships with our patients. The doctor-patient bond is one of deep sharing and trust. No one believes that more than we do. But we also believe that most of the advice and conversations about planning for a honeymoon should and must occur between the couple approaching marriage and their parents, families, pastor *and* a mentor couple.

Unfortunately, these personal and private conversations have been lost in our modern age, but they are as critical for today's brides and grooms as they were during the days of King Solomon.

This book is our attempt to dispense the best of ancient wisdom, sprinkled with the flavoring of a dash of modern medical and counseling advice and mixed with the experiences and stories of others who have gone before you, to allow you to plan and pray not just for your wedding but also for your honeymoon and your marriage.

We believe that if you invest the time and effort to prepare for a special, sacred and spiritual honeymoon, then the fruit of that investment will bless not just your marriage but also, as you share this wisdom with others, the marriages of many who will follow your path.

For Thought and Prayer

1. Based on what you've learned so far, have you or your fiancé had any "wrong ideas" about your honeymoon?

2. Have you found anyone you can talk with about preparing for the honeymoon of a lifetime?

3. For the groom-to-be: Are you willing to take the lead in planning the honeymoon of a lifetime? While your fiancée works overtime to plan *your* wedding, are you willing to invest in her, your marriage and your future by becoming the "lead dog" for this expedition and adventure?

4. How and when do you plan to implement each of these decisions?

Chapter Two

THE DIVINE DESIGN
FOR MARRIAGE

Love is patient, love is kind. It does not envy, it does not boast, it is not proud. It does not dishonor others, it is not self-seeking, it is not easily angered, it keeps no record of wrongs. Love does not delight in evil but rejoices with the truth. It always protects, always trusts, always hopes, always perseveres. Love never fails.

1 CORINTHIANS 13:4-8

Brad and Jill knew from the first moment they saw each other that they were soul mates. "You complete me," he'd tell her. Brad was aptly describing the biblical concept of two becoming one—the divine design for marriage.

Why would we have a chapter on marriage at the beginning of a book about planning the honeymoon of a lifetime? Because your honeymoon will be the foundation for your marriage, and we want you to know that understanding the divine design for your marriage will help you comprehend how beneficial it is to have a divinely designed honeymoon.

As you'll see in the resources recommended at the end of this chapter, there are many useful books written about having a great marriage. So we will review only a few of the basic principles and then focus on the subject of helping you plan your honeymoon of a lifetime.

There Is a Divine Design for Marriage

The Genesis account of creation tells us that after creating Adam, God commented, "It is not good for the man to be alone" (2:18). In order for God's complete image to be revealed in the marriage relationship, the

Creator created Eve to be Adam's counterpart. Men and women were divinely designed to be together as intricately interlocking parts of one whole. Husband and wife were intended to fit together like dovetailed pieces of finely crafted furniture, perfectly fitted together spiritually, relationally, emotionally and physically.

Like a thread weaving throughout the Scriptures, Old and New Testament alike, love is shown to be the root of significance and meaning and purpose—in life and in marriage. In fact, when challenged by a Pharisee (who also happened to be a lawyer) about which of God's commandments was the most important, Jesus referred to Moses' first commandment when He said, "'Love the Lord your God with all your heart and with all your soul and with all your mind.' This is the first and greatest commandment. And the second is like it: 'Love your neighbor as yourself.' All the Law and the Prophets hang on these two commandments" (Matt. 22:37-40).

Because the very essence of God is love, we should not be surprised to find love at the center of the marriage relationship, which was instituted by God. God knew that Adam needed a partner equal in value and complementary in skill, temperament, gifting and design to harmonize with him. In Genesis 2:18, Moses tells us that when God made Eve, He was making "a helper suitable for him [Adam]."

The Hebrew words used here can be translated as an equal or perfect match, dovetailed opposite, or simply a "helper who is just right for him" (*TLB, NIRV*). Regarding these Hebrew words, one scholar has written, "Woman was not intended to be merely man's helper. She was to be instead his partner."[1] Clearly, woman was not created to be a weak or passive counterpart. Rather, the divine design is that a man and woman, in marriage, are equal but complementary parts to a potentially amazing whole.

It's *Not* About You

Katrina was the center of her own personal universe. Her family's life revolved around her every wish and desire. An only child of divorce, she lived up to her daddy's nickname for her: Princess.

Jacob, her fiancé, treated her just like a princess too—after all, that's what she looked for in a man. He even saved up enough money from an extra night job to buy the two-carat, princess-cut, platinum diamond engagement ring that she had chosen for him to give her. It wasn't a great quality diamond, but it was big! He adored her, though, and she adored her ring.

He thought premarital counseling would be a good idea and suggested it, but she complained that she had too much to do to attend to "such trivialities." Jacob had heard from a good friend about the value of spending time with a mentor couple, but Katrina felt the couple he had chosen was "the wrong class of people."

Jacob should have picked up the early warning clues—especially when he was planning their honeymoon. Their two-week European honeymoon and cruise cost tens of thousands of dollars they did *not* have, but Katrina simply would not take no for an answer. On the honeymoon, she insisted on only the best—first-class airfare and restaurants, expensive room service and suites, limousines instead of taxis, etc. You get the picture.

Two years later, Jacob was working three jobs in order to serve Katrina's insatiable appetite for spending and her demands for bigger and better. He was almost never home because he was working all the time. Still he was not able to keep down their credit card debt or even think of affording a down payment for a house. Their marriage ended in divorce when Katrina moved on to another man (sure to be richer and better).

The diamond ring turned out to be a metaphor for their marriage: When your focus is self-centered rather than marriage centered, quality always suffers. Simply put, the divine design is that once you are married, it's no longer all about you. It's about the *one* that the two of you will become together.

If your life has revolved around *your* needs and desires up to this point, then get ready, because things are about to change. From the time you say "I do," life is no longer about just you. It is about your marriage and the two of you walking life's road together, and the family God is forming with you.

If each of you is not prepared to set aside your own selfish desires and commit yourself to working together toward what is best for your marriage, beginning with your honeymoon, then your marriage has very little chance of surviving. We would encourage each of you to consider, even at this late hour, where your priorities are and whether each of you is truly ready to commit to a lifetime of love.

> Do nothing from *selfishness* or empty conceit, but with humility of mind regard one another as more important than yourselves; do not merely look out for your own personal interests, but also for the interests of others (Phil. 2:3-4, *NASB*, emphasis added).

> For where you have envy and *selfish* ambition, there you find disorder and every evil practice (Jas. 3:16, emphasis added).

It's Not Always Easy

Sue's friend Jane had this to say about marriage and dying to self: "When you say 'In sickness and in health,' you sort of think that the sickness part always means someone else. It's rough when it's actually *your* marriage that is affected."

This thought could hold true for any part of the marriage vows: for better or worse, for richer or poorer, in sickness and in health. In marriage, just as in life, there are good times and bad. It's *not* always easy, and when times are difficult, you will not be alone. *Every* marriage is tested by the challenges of life. I tell newlyweds, "If you're not in a storm, hold on, because one's comin'!"

In this book, we'll show you how you can predict and prepare for some of these storms—some of which can even show up during the honeymoon.

It's a Balancing Act

It's a delicate balance, this equal but complementary lifelong relationship between one man and one woman that is divinely designed, God-invented and called marriage.

With two such strong and opposite persons joined together, there had to be a system of authority and governance to make it stay together or it would naturally self-destruct. The divine design is that God would occupy the center of every marriage relationship. He must have realized we would need some guidance on how to keep this delicate equilibrium between husband, wife, and Creator focused and productive. Let's briefly look at God's design and His instructions for a healthy marriage.

In Ephesians 5:21, the Bible recommends that the husband *and* the wife "be subject to one another" (*RSV*). In other words, both of you are instructed to put aside your own selfish desires by serving your Creator first and then by serving one another. This type of servant leadership is not possible humanly speaking. It can only be powered to its unexpected magnitude and impact when fueled by the greatest power of all—the Creator who designed it—as He pours His love in you and through you.

It's About Unconditional Love (Men)

In Ephesians 5:25, we guys are instructed, "Husbands, love your wives, just as Christ loved the church and gave himself up for her." In Ephesians 5:28-30, we are taught, "Husbands ought to love their wives as their own bodies. He who loves his wife loves himself. After all, people have never hated their bodies, but they feed and care for them, just as Christ does the church—for we are members of his body."

Men, we are to love our wives exactly as our Creator loves us. We are to give ourselves in sacrificial love to our wife as Christ gave Himself for us. We are to love our wife as our own body—for indeed she is one with us. Our wives are to be "Job No. 1." Not only is this *not* easy—it's impossible! At least it is in *your* power and strength.

This isn't a man-sized job; it's a God-sized job. It requires God's supernatural love acting in and through us.

Nick thought of himself as the perfect husband. He worked hard, provided for his family and never even considered having an affair. Everyone told Nick's wife, Amber, how lucky she was to have a husband as good and as handsome as Nick. But outsiders couldn't see what was really happening in Nick and Amber's relationship.

On the inside, Amber secretly resented all those long hours that Nick spent working. Sometimes she even felt like a single mom! When Nick came home, he made it clear that the housework and kids were Amber's responsibility and that it was his time to relax. Rarely did he stop to give her a hug or kiss, and she couldn't remember the last time he told her that he loved her. After all, he reasoned, she must know he does. He married her, didn't he? Amber had everything she could possibly want to buy with Nick's hard-earned money. Yet slowly, over time, Amber was feeling more and more isolated and lonely in their marriage.

At this point, Amber and Nick's marriage would be extremely vulnerable to an affair or a divorce. What a shame! There's no abuse or adultery eroding their relationship. This marriage is simply suffering from Nick's neglecting Amber's physical, spiritual and emotional needs—subtle, insidious and damaging, but completely preventable if Nick would simply learn about and demonstrate on a daily basis the divine design for loving his wife. If Nick chooses not to, their marriage relationship could be in real jeopardy.

It's About Unconditional Respect (Women)

A wife has a couple of unique roles in the divinely designed marriage. In Ephesians 5:33, the Bible teaches, "The wife must respect her husband."

While your husband is to unconditionally love you, you are to unconditionally respect him. According to the divine design, respecting your man is to be "Job No. 1." Again, not only is this *not* easy—it's impossible! At least it's impossible in *your* power and strength.

Your man is as divinely designed to respond positively to your unconditional respect and admiration as you are divinely designed to respond to his loving, honoring, nourishing and cherishing care of you.

This isn't a woman-sized job; it's a God-sized job. It requires God's supernatural love.

According to the divine design, as a wife, part of unconditional respect for your husband is to encourage him to provide leadership in your marriage. Now, we know that to some secular progressives and egalitarians, this concept is politically incorrect; however, we both believe deeply that this is an essential part of God's divine design for marriage.

We also know that women are strong, capable and talented—of that there's no doubt. But, ladies, a woman who tries to prove these traits by dominating her husband will actually drive him away. If you choose to dominate him, we believe you may wreck your marriage and destroy your man.

Stacey was a strong woman. She was well educated and gave birth to five children naturally. Anything a man could do, well, *she* could do better. After all, that's how she was raised—and she had opportunities that generations of women before her never dared dream of. Unfortunately for Ned, her husband, just because she was capable of running everything, she failed to realize how much she and her children were divinely designed to really need him in a marriage. Through her nagging, constant disrespect and ridicule, he was beaten down to an ineffective, disengaged, sorry shadow of the husband he could have been to her. It was not a pretty sight.

Don't ruin your marriage by making Nick's or Stacey's mistakes. A better choice is to choose to demonstrate your feminine strength by respecting your husband and encouraging him to lead you and your children. Lift him up when you are with him and speak highly of him when you are with others. Choose to be strong in your support of him— in cheering him on. It's a much more powerful position than it first appears. We could all use a little bit more respect, but men simply cannot live without it—especially from their soul mate.

It's About the Marital Dance

As we were writing this book, a surprisingly popular show *Dancing with the Stars* was on television. The winning couple and two of the final three couples had an amateur male dancing with a female professional ballroom dancer. Was the woman the better dancer? Absolutely! Was she the more talented? No doubt! However, could she have won the contest alone? No way!

David Mills, the editor of *Touchstone* magazine, has penned a beautiful word picture of this divine design for a husband and wife in marriage:

Traditional couples, who have been married a long time, if they've worked at their marriages, work so well together that it's increasingly hard in most matters to distinguish their "sex roles." This is something the egalitarians never understand about hierarchy: that it leads to the thing they think they want but can't get the way they want to get it.

It's as if the couple has spent so long learning to dance that now they move so fast and so smoothly that you just see one thing (one flesh) moving. The husband has always led, and he's still leading, but he's better at it: He's leading his wife where she can and (mostly) wants to go, and she's following because she wants to.

She trusts him and thinks that following him makes the dance better, and even when it doesn't (because he's not perfect), they keep dancing in a way that covers the mistake. If she hesitates or resists, he changes the dance, most of the time (because he's not perfect), because he knows she knows something he doesn't.

Meanwhile, the egalitarian couple, if they're still dancing together, are examining their contract to see who is supposed to be leading now, and for how long, and under what conditions, and with what limits, and making sure the benefits of dancing are shared equally, as are the costs, and when they finally get on the dance floor they have to keep stopping to negotiate all those little points that weren't covered in the contract. There are some egalitarians spinning around the floor, but only because at some point they stopped dancing like egalitarians.

I can understand the egalitarians' point of view and, like them, can think of some of the men still tromping on their wives' feet because they think that leading means dragging and pushing, but I still prefer the dance to the negotiation.[2]

It's About Following the Divine Design

"A person standing alone can be attacked and defeated, but two can stand back-to-back and conquer. Three are even better, for a triple-braided cord is not easily broken" (Eccles. 4:12, *NLT*).

There are lots of scholarly interpretations for this verse about the triple-braided cord. Certainly, it can be considered a case for all kinds of societal units—families, government and churches. However, it is in the context of marriage that this verse holds a secret of significant power.

We have always considered our Creator as the third strand of the cord in our marriages. He is the added strength and stability in our relationship with our spouses. Consistently trusting God to lead our marriages and our families provides both purpose and a firm foundation. In times of conflict (yes, there have been many of those for both us, and there will be for you also), it's important to keep your eyes on God and His divine design for you and your marriage to direct you away from your own selfish points of view—and that can be a marriage saver. The inevitable result of a man and woman growing closer to God is that they grow closer to each other.

It's About Avoiding an Unequal Yoke

My wife, Barb, and I enjoy being able to do premarital counseling with couples. We find that so many couples spend all of their energy and time planning the wedding and virtually no time planning their marriage. By aiming at the smaller and less significant target (the wedding) and taking their eyes off the larger and more difficult-to-hit objective of a lifelong, deeply satisfying and enriching marriage, they are shocked to sorely miss the mark.

A healthy and happy marriage takes a lot of preparation and even more work; but if marriage is attempted by a man and a woman who cannot pull together spiritually in the yoke of marriage, the whole thing is much more likely to end in a wreck.

The divine design for marriage could not be more unmistakably clear—spiritual compatibility between marriage partners is critical—and with good reason: "Don't team up with those who are unbelievers" (2 Cor. 6:14, *NLT*).

If you are currently in an unequal relationship, spiritually or emotionally, we urge you to reconcile those differences prior to committing to a lifetime marriage vow. At the end of this chapter, you will find resources and suggestions to help you work through these issues together.

For Thought and Prayer

Entering into a marriage relationship is no light matter. Here are a couple of questions for you to consider in thought and prayer:

1. Are you marriage material? Do your behaviors, values and the way you live represent what you would want in a partner? If not, ask God to help you in your areas of struggle. Seek forgiveness from God and pray for your future marriage partner. Ask that he or she will pray for you also as you prepare yourself for marriage.

2. Men, are you comfortable loving your wife-to-be in the way described in this chapter? Are you skilled at this? If not, you may want to choose one of the resources listed below and use it to gain knowledge and skills.

3. Women, are you comfortable respecting and following your husband-to-be in the way described in this chapter? Do you have and are you using these skills now? If not, then you may want to choose one of the books at the end of the chapter and use it to gain knowledge and skills.

4. Are you and your partner equally yoked? Do you share the same spiritual foundation and beliefs? If not, this is something you will want to discuss, work through and consider before committing to a lifelong partnership.

5. How and when do you plan to implement each of these decisions?

Resources

We've only briefly touched the surface of the divine design for the marriage relationship between a man and a woman. For a more in-depth study on relationships and marriage, we recommend that you and your fiancé consider reading together one or more of the following:

Chapman, Gary. *The Five Love Languages: How to Express Heartfelt Commitment to Your Mate.* Chicago, IL: Northfield Publishers, 1996.

Eggrichs, Emerson. *Love and Respect: The Love She Most Desires, the Respect He Desperately Needs.* Franklin, TN: Integrity Publishers, 2004.

Parrott, Les, and Leslie Parrott. *Saving Your Marriage Before It Starts: Seven Questions to Ask Before (and After) You Marry.* Grand Rapids, MI: Zondervan Publishing House, 1995.

Rosberg, Gary, and Barbara Rosberg. *Divorce Proof Your Marriage: 6 Secrets to a Forever Marriage.* Carol Stream, IL: Tyndale House Publishers, 2003.

Thomas, Gary L. *Sacred Marriage.* Grand Rapids, MI: Zondervan Publishing House, 2000.

Chapter Three

INVEST IN
STAY-MARRIED
INSURANCE!

For wisdom will enter your heart,
and knowledge will fill you with joy.

PROVERBS 2:10, *NLT*

N ot one person we have counseled before marriage plans to divorce. Not one. Yet, those who choose not to apply the principles contained in this book have a significant chance of seeing their marriage end in a very sad or even traumatic fashion. The Americans for Divorce Reform estimates that chance to be 40 to 50 percent if current social trends continue.[1] No matter the actual percentage, we think you would do anything you could to prevent this possibility, right? Well, of course!

One expert has written that there are eight basic causes of divorce:

1. Money
2. Alcohol
3. Sexual problems
4. Immaturity
5. Jealousy
6. Unreasonable expectations
7. Problems with in-laws
8. Irresponsibility[2]

We believe that many of these causes of divorce can be discovered and dealt with before marriage. So our first topic for your honeymoon (and marriage) of a lifetime is to invest in a bit of what we call stay-married insurance.

What Is Stay-Married Insurance?

Why is it so important to take the time to consider these issues now? And why in the world would we dedicate so much effort to these marriage principles in a book about the honeymoon?

It's simple. The honeymoon is the beginning of the marriage—the beginning of a lifetime relationship between a man and a woman—and we want you to have not only the happiest and healthiest of honeymoons but also the best and most satisfying marriage possible.

We believe that proper honeymoon and marriage preparation is literal stay-married insurance. There are several critical steps you must take now if you want to protect your marriage in the future. Although we could write a chapter about each, let us just briefly introduce them for your consideration.

Devote Time to a Premarital Inventory

For years, I have recommended that the couples Barb and I counsel find a pastor, priest, rabbi or counselor who uses a premarital assessment or a premarital inventory, followed by a number of premarital counseling sessions to explore the results.

Two of the best inventories, in my opinion, are the Premarital Personal and Relationship Evaluation (PREPARE)[3] and Facilitating Open Couple Communication, Understanding and Study (FOCCUS)[4] assessments.

Nine of PREPARE's 11 scales have been shown to predict, with 74 percent to 84 percent accuracy, which couples will divorce.[5] A study of FOCCUS found that of 207 couples, 67.6 percent were correctly classified according to marital quality five years after the inventory was taken.[6]

The PREPARE system is typically used by trained counselors. The FOCCUS system can be used by you, your fiancé and an untrained mentor couple. The FOCCUS system offers follow-up questions that make it easy for a mentor couple to use with you and your fiancé. In addition, FOCCUS is somewhat friendlier to faith-based couples. For example, it has a section called "Marriage Covenant" (which is not in the PREPARE system). This section reviews items such as

- My future spouse and I have discussed the meaning of our marriage commitment to pledge love under all circumstances.
- I believe that God's power can bring life out of struggles and suffering in our marriage.
- I am comfortable asking my future spouse to pray with me.

There is another premarital assessment option, the RELATE system, which is available via the Internet but is not linked to premarital counseling or a mentor couple—which we consider critical in marriage preparation.[7]

It is *far* more preferable for you as an engaged couple to fully discuss any issues an inventory raises with a mentor couple, pastor or counselor. Without the third-party involvement, most difficult issues are simply going to be glossed over—although they will most certainly raise their ugly heads during your honeymoon or marriage. In this arena, an ounce of prevention is worth a ton of cure!

If these inventories are administered 6 to 12 months before the wedding, *and* the couple has numerous feedback sessions with a pastoral professional, faith-based counselor or mentor couple to discuss the issues raised, the couple will be able to discover and deal with many potential problems that could lead to a horrible honeymoon, a miserable marriage or a devastating divorce. And who wants *that?!* Therefore, we think it's important for you and your fiancé to use this preventive medicine and purchase this stay-married insurance *before* your honeymoon and marriage.

My son, Scott, and his then fiancée, Jennifer, used the PREPARE inventory during their courtship in 2005. Scott told me, "Dad, I not only learned tons about Jennifer, but I learned *so* much about myself."[8] With PREPARE, they found several potential areas of conflict and were able to talk and pray about them.

Consider Investing in Professional Premarital Counseling
However, Scott and Jennifer did not *just* use the premarital inventory. They wisely chose to combine it with another critical marriage insurance policy—professional counseling. They used the PREPARE inventory, but only as a start (a foundation) to more in-depth preparation and learning by following up their work on the inventory with eight 60- to 90-minute sessions with their pastor, who was also a trained premarital counselor.

Professional premarital counseling and thorough psychological and spiritual assessments with a trained Christian psychiatrist, psychologist or marriage and family specialist will cost a little more, but it is worth its weight in gold in the long run. Such evaluations include professional evaluation of each spouse-to-be, including mental status, childhood prejudices, marital expectation, personality traits and a host of other factors that can eventually sink a marriage. My good friend, psychiatrist and theologian Paul Meier, MD, says:

> It is often accurately said that whenever two people (like the bride and groom) are present with each other, there are actually six people present: the two as they see themselves, the two as they see each other (idealizations included), and the two as they really are—as only God can see them. Professional premarital therapy and assessment attempts to discover much truth about underlying motivations, hidden sociopathic or personality disorders, etc. In some cases it may contribute to the couple actually breaking off their engagement or putting off their wedding, but usually it strengthens the couple's commitment to each other as they understand each other better and have more realistic expectations of each other and themselves.[9]

Dr. Meier has worked with hundreds of couples for premarital assessments during his career. He writes the following about Sally, one of his clients:

Sally grew up with a father who was severely abusive to her, physically and verbally, and very controlling. And so, like the majority of women who grow up like this, she was only attracted all her life to guys who were controlling and abusive, because she had huge blind spots. Unconsciously, she wanted to fix her father. She was so used to abuse that she missed it when it was not happening, and—like most abuse victims—had low self-esteem and felt like she deserved the abuse.

When Sally and Jack went through professional counseling at my clinic, Sally was shocked to find out that this man, who she thought was nice and wonderful, was actually a controlling and abusive sociopath and a con man who would have been a disaster for her when she said "I do."

Sally's "people picker" was broken. But, continuing therapy after she and Jack called off their engagement enabled her to see the truth about her own unconscious need to win her father's approval, or a substitute father like Jack.[10]

Regarding their significant investment of money and time, my daughter-in-law, Jennifer, says, "The premarital testing educated us on some potential areas of conflict, and our counselor worked with us to work through these and develop some realistic expectations . . . these sessions also gave us a safe environment in which we could discuss our expectations with a mediator. Otherwise, we wouldn't have had that help."[11]

Invest in Premarital Financial Preparation

One area that almost always surfaces in premarital counseling is the different views and beliefs a couple has about finances and spending—and there are likely to be *huge* differences here.

Fortunately, there are a number of resources available to assist couples in working through these issues.[12] One young groom told me that learning about financial principles before marriage "was huge for helping us to establish our first ever (for both of us) budget. We're four years into it, and it has provided a solid base and guideline for us to continue to move more aggressively into our financial stewardship and desires. Without dealing with financial issues and philosophy before our marriage, we would have had many, many more problems both during our honeymoon and our marriage."

Barb and I have benefited from the weekend and small-group courses and materials of Crown Financial Ministries. Couples we have counseled have obtained great advice from Crown and from the material published by Dave Ramsey.

No matter which financial preparedness information you choose, don't put off doing this before the wedding.

Attend a Premarital Conference

I also recommend that engaged couples consider attending at least one weekend conference for fiancés.[13] Although this step is likely not a critical one, it can serve to give you two an opportunity to discuss the issues you discover in the first two steps alone and with other engaged couples. Barb and I have been particularly fond of the impact that the Family Life Conferences (A Weekend to Remember) have had on our marriage. But couples we have counseled have also greatly benefited from Engaged Encounter Weekends.

Find a Mentor Couple

Last, but not least, find a mentor couple to help mentor you through your honeymoon and marriage. Don't *consider* finding one—don't *think* about finding one—don't *meditate* on finding one—find one! One ministry that provides trained marriage mentors for engaged couples is Marriage Savers.[14]

Usually, a pastor or counselor who uses one of the premarital assessments will only take an hour or so to review the more than 150 items. Trained mentor couples will work through every item of your assessment, complimenting you where you both are in agreement, while discussing those items that may be a problem or about which you two disagree.

Mike and Harriet McManus, the founders of Marriage Savers, have trained mentor couples in their local church and across the country. Harriet believes that the mentor couple has at least three great gifts to offer an engaged couple:

- First, "they provide premarital couples with their unconditional love, a love that grows out of a joy in their own marriage, and out of gratitude to God for that blessing."[15]

- Second, "they offer their time. . . . Mentor couples will typically spend 2 to 3 hours each meeting with one couple for six sessions."[16] Twelve to 18 hours allows ample time to discuss many issues in depth. Compare this major investment with the fact that two-thirds of clergy offer no premarital inventory, and those who do, devote only an hour or two discussing it.

- Third, Harriet asserts, "Mentor couples offer the gift of their own marriage—an imperfect but healthy marital role model for a premarital couple. They are a walking parable of keys to marital success as well as pitfalls to be avoided."[17]

A Mentor Couple's Goals
The goals of a mentor couple are as follows:

- To facilitate discussion of the issues that surfaced in your and your fiancé's premarital inventory,

- To model and help you and your fiancé develop healthy communication skills,

- To encourage you and your fiancé to learn to find *your* solutions to *your* problems,

- To help you and your fiancé learn how to prepare a budget and set goals,

- To encourage your and your fiancé's spiritual growth, and

- To share personal marital wisdom.

We need to emphasize that mentor couples do not have to have (and, in fact, will never have) a perfect marriage. They only need to be willing to share their marital journey and help facilitate your learning skills in communication and problem solving. In our opinion, the strongest mentor couples are those who understand that a strong marriage requires great effort and a reliance on God as a third partner.

The Benefits of Having a Mentor Couple
The benefits of having a mentor couple include the following:

- They give you a real-life sounding board and a role model.

- They can give you assurance that you've made a wise choice for a spouse.

- They can give you assurance that your risk for divorce will be significantly diminished.

- They can enhance your future honeymoon and marriage.

My daughter-in-law, Jennifer, wrote, "Having a mentor couple during our engagement was a *huge* supplement to our premarital counseling. Chuck and Jenny gave us a living example of a family with similar values. We could meet informally and ask question after question—which was especially important during or after arguments! They weren't professional counselors, but they were experts at loving us and demonstrating, in their home, what marriage is truly all about."[18]

During the past decade, 288 engaged couples were mentored in the McManus's church. The shocker in their program was that 53 of these couples (more than 18 percent) decided *not* to marry. At first blush, this might appear to be a much higher breakup rate than is normal—as much, perhaps, as 10 times that of an average church. However, Mike McManus reports, "Studies show that those who break an engagement after taking a premarital inventory have the same scores as those who marry and later divorce. Thus, these 53 couples avoided a bad marriage before it even began."[19]

What happened to the other 235 couples? Only seven divorced within a decade. That's a divorce rate of about 3 percent. Folks, that's *great* marriage insurance!

Any faith community can offer this type of marriage insurance, if it (1) requires all marrying couples to use a premarital inventory, (2) requires all marrying couples to prepare financially, and (3) provides mentor couples for all engaged couples.

Marriage Savers has also persuaded 10,000 rabbis, pastors, priests and other clergy in more than 200 cities to sign a Community Marriage Policy in which most of a city's clergy require the taking of a premarital inventory with trained mentor couples. Why? Many engaged couples simply don't think they need rigorous marriage prep, and they will avoid a church with such requirements to get married in one where they only have to meet with the pastor once or twice. Does a Community Marriage Policy make a difference? You bet! In fact, in each of these cities, divorce rates have plummeted.

For example, in Austin, Texas (a liberal community, by Texas standards), 252 churches agreed to a Community Marriage Policy requiring the inventory and mentoring. So premarital couples who want a church wedding in Austin have to take this more rigorous preparation. The result? Austin's divorce rate fell 50 percent from 1996, when it was signed, through 2001, according to the Institute for Research and Evaluation.[20]

Marriage Savers has also trained more than 3,000 mentor couples in more than 1,000 churches to make marriage preparation far more rigorous across a whole community. You can learn more about stay-married insurance at the Marriage Savers website.[21]

Another ministry that helps churches and couples prepare for marriage is Right Start.[22]

If you can't find a trained mentor couple, consider checking with your pastor to see whether he has a couple he can recommend for you. Or if there's a happily married couple you know and trust, approach them about mentoring you and your fiancé. Both you and your mentor couple could get Marriage Saver information and the FOCCUS inventory and learn together![23] By the way, Marriage Savers uses FOCCUS (instead of PREPARE) because, according to Mike McManus, "it is more mentor friendly." The mentor couple uses a FOCCUS Facilitator Notebook listing inventory items on the left side of the page, with helpful follow-up questions to the right.

A Warning

Investing in a premarital inventory, premarital counseling, premarital financial education and planning, and time with a mentor couple is a lot of hard work—no doubt about it. What if you, or your fiancé, are not willing to intentionally prepare for your marriage by doing this work? A wise person has written:

> When a young man is irresponsible and unwilling to work before marriage, the chances are extremely good that he'll continue the same pattern of behavior after marriage. In the same way the young lady who has shown no sense of personal responsibility before marriage will likely also be unwilling to do her part in (maintaining) the home after marriage.
>
> If you're planning to marry such a person, with the expectation of changing him or her, it is very likely that you're in for a sad disappointment. Regardless of how sincerely one may promise to change after marriage, it is very unlikely that such a person will suddenly alter the habits of a lifetime.[24]

However, if *both* of you are willing to make the investment in these insurance policies, no matter which approach or system you choose, we believe that you will be well prepared not only for your honeymoon but also for a lifelong marriage.

Recently, Edna and Charles celebrated their sixtieth wedding anniversary. She was stunningly beautiful, with her silvery hair and peacock-blue silk dress. The sparkle in her eye offered a glimpse into the heart of a woman far younger than her current years. They were so cute, and so obviously still in love, staying by each other's side and holding each other's hand throughout the evening. When asked for the secret of their marriage's longevity, Charles replied with a charming grin, "We're still on our honeymoon."

Oh, that we could all be so blessed! There is great joy in a balanced, loving relationship centered on God's divine design for husbands and wives.

For Thought and Prayer

Entering into a marriage relationship is no light matter. Here are some questions for you to consider in thought and prayer:

1. Are you and your fiancé willing to invest in stay-married insurance?

2. Are you and your fiancé willing to look for and begin premarital counseling with a pastoral professional or marriage and family counselor? An equally yoked marriage will literally influence everything in your life together, especially whether your marriage will survive.

3. Are you and your fiancé willing to use a premarital system and participate in significant premarital counseling?

4. Are you and your fiancé willing to find and begin meeting with a mentor couple?

5. Do you and your fiancé need to go through some financial training and education?

6. Do you and your fiancé desire to attend a marriage preparation conference?

7. How and when do you plan to implement each of these decisions?

Resources

PREPARE-ENRICH Premarital Inventory. www.prepare-enrich.com/ indexm.cfm

FOCCUS Premarital Inventory. www.foccusinc.com/

RELATE Premarital Inventory. www.relate-institute.org/

Crown Financial Ministry. www.crown.org/

Dave Ramsey. www.daveramsey.com/

Engaged Encounter. www.marriage.about.com/od/engagedencounter/

Weekend to Remember. www.familylife.com/conferences/marriage.asp

Marriage Savers. www.marriagesavers.org

Chapter Four

SAFE SEX? SAVE SEX!

When you lie down, you will not be afraid;
when you lie down, your sleep will be sweet.

PROVERBS 3:24

In the Bible, the phrase "lie down" is often used to indicate sexual intimacy—and nowhere in medicine, in our experience, except in the case of the diagnosis of cancer or other life-threatening illnesses, have we seen more anxiety than that surrounding sexual behavior.

Certainly, when it comes to preventive medicine, fear regarding sexual issues tops the list. Think about it. Why would the National Institutes for Health (NIH) need a phrase such as "safe sex" or "safer sex" to describe sexual practices if it wasn't somehow potentially unsafe or dangerous?

What If I Have Concerns About Sex?

In our medical practices, we have seen just about everything that relates to fear of sex! Fear of having too much sex—or not enough. Fear of being hurt, embarrassed, harassed or assaulted. Fear of performance problems. Fear of getting pregnant—unintentionally, out of wedlock, or just in general. Fear of not getting pregnant. Fear of sexually transmitted diseases or infections, vaginitis, bladder infections, libido problems, birth control issues, and the list goes on and on.

Our practices span the gamut of society, from the jails and drug-infested inner cities to rural America to Olympic and professional athletes to high-society celebrities, politicians and VIPs. Take it from two doctors who have seen it up close and personal, sexual concerns know no social, ethnic, religious or political boundaries!

Does it seem odd to include a section like this in a book about honeymoons? After all, a honeymoon is supposed to be a happy time. It's about love and joy and happiness—not about fear. Well, we have included this section because we want your honeymoon to be the beginning of the happiest marriage possible, so we need to present some information about sexual health issues.

It is our prayer that you not be anxious about anything on your honeymoon and in your marriage, especially regarding sexual intimacy. And we have great news for you! Even though you may have concerns about sex as you begin your marriage (and almost *everybody* does have concerns), it's going to be fine! No, not just fine, but potentially great! That's part of the divine design for your honeymoon and marriage.

Your honeymoon is going to be great not only because it will so mightily affect your marriage but also because you will, for the first time, experience the physical joy of being with another to whom you've pledged your lifelong, undying love and to whom you are joined not just physically, emotionally, relationally and legally—but also spiritually.

There can be exceeding freedom and peace in this place of oneness. There can be incredible joy—even if every detail doesn't turn out as you had planned or hoped. It's going to be great because you two will be alone together (finally!) *and* married. The combination is potent—and divinely designed to be so. It can be great whether or not you actually have intercourse with simultaneous orgasms or anything more complicated, simply because you will be together as designed and intended—committed, in love, and with each other.

And we've got more good news. As we researched this book and accumulated the wisdom of hundreds of married couples, one thing we heard over and over again is this: As wonderful as that first night is together, it gets better and better over time, as you grow in your marriage in love and knowledge of each other.

That's right. Our prayer for you is that in 10 . . . 20 . . . 50 . . . years, you will look back on your honeymoon with very warm and happy memories; but beyond the honeymoon, you will smile with the knowing smile of those who have the kind of incredible sex life that is only experienced by those who have dwelt in the richness and fullness of a long and happy marriage—marinated in divinely designed love.

What Is the Definition of Safe Sex?

We went searching for definitions of "safe sex" and found plenty, including (apparently) the latest kind of sex, "*safer* sex." Here are some samples:

- Engaging in sexual activity using measures such as latex condoms to avoid contracting a sexually transmitted disease (STD) such as AIDS.[1]

- Safe sex means taking precautions during sex that can keep you from getting an STD or from giving an STD to your partner. These diseases include genital herpes, genital warts, HIV, chlamydia, gonorrhea, syphilis, hepatitis B and C, and others.[2]

- Safe sex, also called "safer sex" and "protected sex," is a set of practices designed to reduce the risk of transmitting sexually transmitted infections (STIs), also known as sexually transmitted diseases (STDs). Conversely, unsafe sex refers to engaging in sex without the use of any contraceptive or preventive measures against STDs. Safe sex practices became prominent in the late 1980s as a result of the AIDS epidemic. From the viewpoint of society, safer sex can be regarded as a harm-reduction strategy. Safe sex is about risk reduction, not complete risk elimination.[3]

It's almost as if they are saying that dangerous sex (unsafe sex) is any sex without a condom or sex involving the exchange of bodily fluids. Yet, they *never* tell you about the dangers of what they euphemistically call safe sex. They don't tell you how often condoms fail.[4] They don't tell you how you can still contract many forms of sexually transmitted infections, such as human papillomavirus (HPV), even if the condom works well.[5]

And they by no means tell you that a condom *never* protects your heart, soul or brain—all of which are critical in having the best sex of all.

Simply put, the definitions for "safe sex" or "safer sex" are only necessary for men and women who either have chosen to rebel against or simply do not know the divine design for the best sex—love-filled sex. The story is told of a teenaged boy who was talking with his grandfather about safe sex. "Grandpa," he said, "at school they told us wearing a condom was the safest for sex." The old man looked down at his left hand and pointed to the ring that had been on his fourth finger for many decades. "This, son, is all you need to wear for sex. And if you wait until it's properly on, you'll have the best sex possible."

The good news is, you and your fiancé are about to enter into a lifetime of not only the best sex of all, but also the safest sex of all—what God intended as *the* safe sex: that between a mutually monogamous man and woman who are married for life—and you *can* lie down with each and not only *not* be afraid but also be filled with trust, satisfaction and love. Just think—no fear, no condoms, no latex dental dams. Woo-hoo!

Sex *Is* Better in Marriage!

You mean sex gets better with marriage? you may wonder. *But, what about all those stereotypical sitcoms about how sex is only sexy for the young and single swingers? What about all those boring scenarios of separate twin beds, frumpy wives with headaches and beer-bellied husbands watching endless sports?*

We're here to tell you they've got it all wrong! It's an urban legend spread by the sitcoms and soaps. It's a delusional and dangerous myth—a far-fetched fairy tale and fable—fabrication and fiction at its worst.

One of the best kept secrets in America is that the *best* sex is not found in the night clubs of Las Vegas or Los Angeles or New York, not in the singles bars or on university campuses, not even on the beaches of Miami or Hawaii. The best sex is not in the city or on Wisteria Lane. Nope, the most satisfying sex in America is right where you are heading—in the bedrooms of people who are married for life.

Don't believe it? Check out the data yourself. In a famous sex survey conducted by the University of Chicago, the findings regarding the typical American sex life were rather astounding.[6]

Frequency of Sex in the Past Year (Percentage)			
Frequency of Sex	2 or More Times per Week	A Few Times per Month	Not at All to a Few Times per Year
Total population	26–30	36–37	28–30
Married adults	32–36	43–47	14–15

To summarize the overall pattern, American adults fall roughly into three levels of activity in partnered sex: They are either having sex with their partner at least 2 or more times a week, a few times a month, or only a few times a year or not at all. Only in the latter and most sexually boring category (no sex or sex only a few times per year) do non-married adults rate *higher* than their married counterparts. In other words, married couples have sex far more frequently than single or cohabiting adults.[7] But, even more surprising is the following fact.

Sex *Is* Better with Religious or Spiritual Couples

Furthermore, this same study found that the more religious a married couple is, the more frequent and satisfying their sex. That's right! Religious people who are married, by far and away have the best sex lives. They have the most frequent sex, the most satisfying sex, the most fun sex and the longest-lived sex lives.

If this type of sex life was available in a pill, it would outsell Viagra, Levitra and Cialis (the pills used to treat erectile dysfunction in men) combined!

When the researchers looked at which religious denominations had the best sex, they learned that the faithful who are married don't just get excited in church. Not only was their sex more frequent, but also they were far more likely to report their sex as being extremely satisfying.

Conservative evangelical Protestant women, the survey found, reported the most satisfying sex and the most orgasms: Thirty-two percent said they achieve orgasm *every* time they make love. Mainline Protestants and Catholics were only five points behind, while those with no religious affiliation were way down at 22 percent.[8] Ouch! Looks like the *Saturday Night Live* character of the Church Lady may be more fiction than fact, more absurdity than actuality.

Sex Is *Not* Better If You Cohabit

The most dangerous myth of all may be the myth that living together before marriage will result in a better marriage. As a result, in the past 30 years, the number of couples who live together before marriage has increased 1,000 percent. In fact, cohabitation has become so commonplace in our society that a couple who doesn't live together before tying the knot is, in many areas, a cultural anomaly. So why should a couple defy the societal norm by avoiding cohabitation?

There are many important reasons, which David Gudgel fully discusses in his insightful book *Before You Live Together*.[9] Perhaps the most devastating reason, according to Mr. Gudgel, is this: "Of eight couples that live together before marriage, four of them will split up and they will not marry. Of the four that marry, three of them will divorce."[10] Double ouch!

Not only does the cohabiting couple have less frequent sex and less satisfying sex, but they are far more likely, if they eventually do get married, to experience a violent, traumatic and failed marriage. Understanding this will help you understand some of our premarital counseling recommendations later in this book.

What does the marriage of a religious man and woman have to offer a sex life that's so much better than the single life—or even a nonspiritual or nonmonogamous marriage?

Here are our top 10 reasons that sex is better in a faithful, mutually monogamous marriage:

10. Bedrooms are more comfortable than the backseat of a car
    or a borrowed bed.

9. No worries about catching a sexually transmitted infection—ever.

8. Confidence that no matter how you look in the morning, your spouse will still love you and be there in the morning!

7. A few years of your spouse practicing to make *you* happy pays much bigger dividends than a couple of dates in the sack.

6. No trouble finding someone to sleep with—sex more often and more consistently than your unmarried or nonreligious counterparts—and with someone you trust and who is committed to *you* and co-committed with you to God.

5. Have an occasional little sexual malfunction? No judgment. Your spouse knows you're good for another time.

4. Never having to get up and get dressed in yesterday's clothes.

3. No guilt or sneaking around.

2. No worries about having a pregnancy without a spouse, and having both a mother *and* a father for your children.

And the number one reason that sex is better in a spiritual marriage:

1. Because God made it that way, and He judged it as good—very, very good.

So if you had any hesitation about whether you were missing out on something sexually by making this decision to marry, put that worry to rest. And if you've chosen to give away the gift of your virginity to your spouse-for-life after the wedding ceremony and not before, all the better. It's definitely a club worth joining.

What Is Your Most Important Sexual Organ?

Q: What is the most important human sexual organ? Hmmm . . .

A: Your brain, of course! (What *were* you thinking?)

Regardless of the status of any other organ in your body, as long as your brain is still working, your ability to experience sexual pleasure in partnership with your spouse is still possible. This is an issue that comes up commonly in our practices, both in aging populations and in patients with missing or nonfunctional reproductive parts, such as post-hysterectomy patients, patients with severe diabetes, and some cancer survivors. Now, certainly not everyone with these conditions suffers from sexual organ dysfunction, but our point is that sexuality is about so much more than just body parts.

Here lies a key to why it is so important that you pick a lifetime spouse on grounds more solid than physical attraction and with qualities that will see you through the twists and turns that sexuality takes along the course of an entire life lived together. The brain truly is the sexiest organ of them all, and if you don't like your fiancé's personality, how he or she treats you, or his or her attitude, then this person is not going to seem sexy for long, no matter how hot his or her body is!

The idea of strong human sex drive and the consideration of sex outside the boundaries of marriage is not an issue new to the modern era. In fact, since human sexual drive was such an issue even in ancient times, the Bible taught that "since sexual immorality is occurring, each man should have sexual relations with his own wife, and each woman with her own husband" (1 Cor. 7:2).

Your Creator knows about sex drive—after all, it's part of His divine design, and it's His gift to you. Because He knows how strong the sex drive He invented can be, He created a relationship in which He means you to use it—I'm talking about the marriage relationship. If you've had trouble controlling your sexual desires, then you are headed in the right direction, toward marriage. As the Bible says, "If they cannot control themselves, they should marry, for it is better to marry than to burn with passion" (1 Cor. 7:9).

Is There Sex in the Bible?

Sex—isn't that the first thing men *and* women think of when it comes to the honeymoon? And why not? It's the physical confirmation of everything spiritually joined during the wedding ceremony.

To the Creator we must say, "You did a splendid job when You thought up this one." But for something intended to be so incredible, it sure is a gift that can be misused and bring its share of problems!

Is this what was intended in the divine design for sex? Surely not! You may not believe just how much discussion there is about sex in the Bible.

Sex in the Bible? Oh, yes!

Have you read Song of Solomon? *As an adult?* It's that little chapter two books past Proverbs in the Old Testament. *Hello* . . . it's sex, sex, sex. We promise you'll never think of a garden in the same way again after reading a bit of that book. To that end, we recommend reading *Solomon's Song of Love* by Dr. Craig Glickman.[11] It's an absolutely fantastic book on the Song of Solomon in which great advice on love, marriage and sex is given as the reader is guided through the song. Dr. Glickman is recognized as one of the world's top scholars on this book of the Bible—but his book is also great fun to read.

Ahem. Where were we? Oh, yes. The divine design for sex . . .

In all His wisdom, when the Creator granted us this most precious gift, He also saw fit to provide us with some recommendations for enjoying it. Follow these recommendations and there is tremendous freedom sprinkled with great fun, satisfaction and enjoyment.

What Are the Creator's Recommendations for Sex?

1. Abstain from *all* sexual activity until married.
2. Have great sex with your spouse, and *only* your spouse, once you are married.
3. Don't have sex with anyone else—ever.
4. Don't have thoughts about having sex with anyone else, and control your media habits.

Let's briefly examine each of these.

Reserve Sex for Marriage
Yes, that means before, during, after or in between marriages. Statistically, we realize that only some of you reading this book will be virgins when you marry. (We define virgins as men or women who have not

participated in sexual activity before marriage, including sex play involving the genitals, oral sex and genital intercourse—vaginal or anal.) The good news is that the number of virgins is on the rise among young people as more and more of them are choosing the benefits of sexual purity (abstinence) over sexual activity.

Obviously, in writing about refraining from sexual activity until you are married, we risk alienating the large number of you who have already experimented sexually, in one form or fashion, or may in fact be sexually active or even cohabiting now, during your engagement. Not to worry, we have much practical advice for you in our next chapter.

We suspect that it's likely that many of you were simply not taught the incredible benefits of saving sexual activity for marriage. Others of you were falsely led to believe that participating in sexual activity would make you and your future spouse more compatible—that sexual experience would make you a better marriage partner.

Some have been led to believe that sexual activity without actually having sexual intercourse would allow them to remain virgins. And, unfortunately, a few of you have been forced into sexual activity against your will and are living with the terrible wounds of having been sexually abused.

Regardless of your prior sexual history, *now* you are preparing to marry the love of your life and embark upon a lifetime of love that can begin with the honeymoon of a lifetime. *Now* you are setting the stage to enter the covenant of marriage that includes a physical as well as a relational, an emotional *and* a spiritual bond that you have not previously experienced, even if you are sexually experienced.

If you are currently challenged by your desires for each other, particularly if you have a long engagement scheduled, you may want to consider moving up the wedding date. It's certainly worth considering—and we've both had friends and patients who have done so. The wedding does not have to be fancy. You can plan fancy later. Get married. Don't play with the gift of sex outside of the boundaries of marriage.

We could not recommend more strongly that if you're having sex with your fiancé, then stop all sexual activity until your wedding night *and* consider moving the wedding night up. Your marriage is *much* more important than your wedding. We'll discuss the reasons in more depth in the section on secondary virginity in the next chapter.

Let's face it. Any previous sexual experience, even with your fiancé, is nothing more than a dim replica or counterfeit of the real thing—the lifetime of love you are *now* preparing for in marriage.

So *now* is the time for you to reflect on your values and prior choices regarding sexuality and *now* is the time to deal with any emotional baggage. We recommend that you do *not* take that kind of baggage on your honeymoon!

The stakes are high. The issue here is the state of your heart and soul (mind, emotions and will) in preparation for your marriage and your honeymoon.

Have Sex with Your Spouse

Jerrie was one of Sue's favorite patients. She was a sweet young woman from a good family, recently married to a man who was equally handsome and spiritual. She had remained a virgin until her marriage, saving that special part of herself for her husband. Six months into her marriage, she came in to talk. Despite their physical desires for each other, and otherwise fabulous relationship, she was still "saving herself."

It happens more often than you would think.

No, it wasn't that they didn't know what to do—they had figured that part out. And it didn't seem to be a physical problem with either one of them. Simply put, Jerrie had been raised to believe that sex was dirty and not something that good girls did. No matter how much she intellectually believed that sex was okay now that she was married, she had such a distorted view of what a healthy sexual relationship is that even what God meant for good between her and her husband was inconceivable to her.

In counseling Jerrie, an important breakthrough happened in her heart when discussing the following passage from the Bible:

> The husband should not deprive his wife of sexual intimacy, which is her right as a married woman, nor should the wife deprive her husband. The wife gives authority over her body to

her husband, and the husband also gives authority over his body to his wife. So do not deprive each other of sexual relations. The only exception to this rule would be the agreement of both husband and wife to refrain from sexual intimacy for a limited time, so they can give themselves more completely to prayer. Afterward they should come together again so that Satan won't be able to tempt them because of their lack of self-control (1 Cor. 7:3-5, *NLT*).

Yes, the divine design is for the husband and wife to have regular sex as a healthy part of a great marriage. As Jerrie read this, her eyes were opened. She began to realize that not only did she have God's permission to enjoy sex with her husband, but also that He had, in fact, designed her for that purpose. As a couple, they have now come to know the joy of fully sharing themselves with each other in a trusting, sexually intimate relationship, as God intended.

Jerrie's case illustrates one of two extremes regarding marital problems with sexuality that are common in our practices. The other extreme, that of sexual self-indulgence, is certainly the more common. Neither extreme is what God intended. When not properly dealt with, either extreme can wreck a marriage faster than most anything else.

Don't Have Sex with Anyone but Your Spouse

This may seem obvious, but in order to keep the joy and freedom of sex in marriage, this rule is pretty darn important. Without it, risks of sexually transmitted infections and questions of paternity of an unexpected pregnancy become a reality of nightmarish proportions, not to mention the emotional, relational and spiritual damage that a cheating spouse can do to an engagement or marriage.

In preparation for your marriage, you should give additional deep thought and prayer to this issue: Do you trust your fiancé now? Should he or she trust you? If you have trust issues in your relationship now, we urge you either to reconsider your plans to marry or to seek professional counseling to resolve these issues so that you can build a firm foundation for your life together.

If you do not fully trust each other before marriage, it's likely that you will not fully trust one another in marriage. Period.

Don't Have Thoughts About Having Sex with Anyone but Your Spouse
The Bible teaches that "anyone who looks at a woman lustfully has already committed adultery with her in his heart" (Matt. 5:28).

Whoa! My thoughts? You mean God's going to hold me accountable for my thoughts? Yikes! That's a tough one.

We think this is probably one of the most difficult truths about God's divine design concerning sex. After all, how hard is it to control a fleeting thought across your mind? These kinds of thoughts may happen without any conscious decision to go there at all, which is why limiting your exposure to sexually explicit materials—movies, pornography, sexually explicit reading materials—becomes so important. It's difficult to control our thoughts; but if we don't put the images there to begin with, the thoughts are not as difficult to control.

Why is this issue of our thoughts concerning sex so important? The Bible explains that it's our thoughts that influence our actions. It's our thoughts that are at the root of anything not right in our behavior, and it's from our thoughts that darkness has a chance to take root—if we let it.

Jesus uses two words for sexual activity with anyone or anything other than your spouse: "Adultery" is nonspousal sexual activity when you *are* married, and "sexual immorality," translated "fornication" in other versions of the Bible, is sexual activity when you are *not* married. Both words are described by Jesus as "evil thoughts" (Mark 7:21).

The Greek word translated "sexual immorality" or "fornication" is *porneia*—the root from which we get the word "pornography." In the Bible, *porneia* and related words also have a figurative meaning of unfaithfulness to God. In other words, fornication is a sin against God, ourselves and our future spouse, while adultery is sin against God, ourselves and our current spouse. Either activity can occur in thought *or* action.

The reason it is so important to take control of our thoughts is that our thoughts control our actions and choices. Adultery and sexual immorality *always* originate in our thoughts and result in activity that more than likely we will deeply regret. It's certainly not the love we want and for which we are designed, and it's not what *any* of us wants for our marriage.

Because we are human, and all of us have less than godly thoughts that cross our minds, how should we overcome these thoughts? First of all, make a decision *now* not to entertain thoughts of sexual activity with anyone other than your spouse.

Treasure your fiancé. Put him or her first and foremost in your thoughts and refrain from purposely looking at members of the opposite sex in a sexual manner, fantasizing about sex with others or viewing sexually explicit material. Simply put, men, when you dwell on and mull over sexual material, you are having an emotional affair. You are having mental sexual activity without your spouse. If you are married, you are committing mental adultery; if you are not married, you are committing mental fornication.

Do whatever you need to do to take control of this issue in your life, especially if you are dealing with attraction to or addiction to pornography. Don't think, *Well, just a little bit won't hurt.* It will hurt! Put controls on your Internet browser, install firewalls and spam blockers. We particularly like the Internet filter Bsafe Online.[12] Bsafe will allow you to designate a mentor or close friend who will receive an e-mail of all the places you've visited on the Internet.

Do whatever you must, but take care of this issue before getting married because it is a potential problem that corrodes the trust and love in marriage, and it can rot a marital relationship from its very core.

Second, ask your Creator to help you with this area. When dealing with an issue, one habit that a lot of people find helpful is to print out Scriptures or other words of encouragement and post them in the car, the office or even on the mirror. Here are three Scriptures that you might find helpful if you need encouragement in this area of your life.

> But the fruit of the Spirit is love, joy, peace, patience, kindness, goodness, faithfulness, gentleness and self-control. Against such things there is no law (Gal. 5:22-23).

Fix your thoughts on what is true and honorable and right. Think about things that are pure and lovely and admirable. Think about things that are excellent and worthy of praise (Phil. 4:8, *NLT*).

Let heaven fill your thoughts. Do not think only about things down here on earth (Col. 3:2, *NLT*).

Now that we've reviewed the divine design for sex in marriage, what should you do if you have already crossed one or more of those barriers? Does crossing a barrier mean that your future sex life is doomed? The answer to that question depends on how you deal with the potentially marriage-saving information in the next chapter.

For Thought and Prayer

1. Take a moment and consider your ideas about sexuality in marriage before you read this chapter. How have your expectations for your sex life as a married couple changed since reading the chapter?

2. What fears do you have about sex? Take a moment to write them down. Then pray and meditate upon each one, asking your Creator to help you work through your fears, removing them before your honeymoon. If you can't get over your fear(s), find a faith-sensitive counselor who can give you some help.

3. What concerns does your fiancé have about sex? Set a time to sit down and talk with each other about the issues regarding sex that exist now in your relationship and how you plan on supporting each other in working toward a sex life without fear.

4. How and when do you plan to implement each of these decisions?

Resources

Crabb, Larry. *The Marriage Builder.* Grand Rapids, MI: Zondervan Publishing House, 1992.

Glickman, *Craig. Solomon's Song of Love.* West Monroe, LA: Howard Books, 2003.

Harley, Willard F., Jr. *His Needs, Her Needs: Building an Affair-Proof Marriage.* Grand Rapids, MI: Revell, 2001.

LaHaye, Tim, and Beverly LaHaye. *The Act of Marriage.* Grand Rapids, MI: Zondervan Publishing House, 1998.

Nelson, Tommy. *The Book of Romance: What Solomon Says About Love, Sex, and Intimacy.* Nashville, TN: Nelson Books, 1998.

Smalley, Gary, and Norma Smalley. *For Better or for Best.* Grand Rapids, MI: Zondervan Publishing House, 1996.

———. *Hidden Keys of a Loving, Lasting Marriage.* Grand Rapids, MI: Zondervan Publishing House, 1993.

———. *If Only He Knew: What No Woman Can Resist.* Grand Rapids, MI: Zondervan Publishing House, 1997.

Smalley, Gary, Greg Smalley, Michael Smalley, and Robert S. Paul. *The DNA of Relationships.* Carol Stream, IL: Tyndale House Publishers, 2004.

Wangerin, Walter, Jr. *As for Me and My House.* Nashville, TN: Nelson Books, 2001.

Chapter Five

FROM PAST SEX TO PERFECT LOVE

If we claim to be without sin, we deceive ourselves and the truth is not in us. If we confess our sins, he is faithful and just and will forgive us our sins and purify us from all unrighteousness.

1 JOHN 1:8-9

If you and your fiancé are among that distinct (although growing) minority of men and women who are both virgins at marriage, give yourselves a high five and move on to the next chapter (although you might want to read the section on perfect love).

However, if you are the average man or woman, then it is quite likely that you have been sexually active in the past—either willfully or against your will—and the vast majority of you are sexually active now. Nevertheless, if one or both of you is, or has ever been, sexually active—in other words, one or both of you is not a virgin—then we recommend that you both read this chapter and get ready to deal with some very difficult issues.

Your Sexual Past

You have an incredible opportunity to prepare for your marriage if you will take the time to assess your personal history regarding past sexual encounters and put the past behind you—if you have been sexually active or have had an overactive sexual thought life—by committing yourself to secondary virginity until your wedding night.

Whatever pain you may have gone through in the past—sexual assault, promiscuity, immorality, fornication, pornography, sexual abuse—these *all* are subject to the healing powers of prayer and forgiveness. These things do not have to enter your marriage relationship. The Bible gives us the assurance and the hope that we can put the past behind us and move on with life once we learn a healthier way to live. You may need to do some of this work individually or with the help of a trained professional counselor, pastor, priest or rabbi.

We have one very strong word of caution: It is not necessarily healthy or essential to disclose *every* detail of your past sexual history to your partner. Please consider what you will disclose only after considerable thought, counsel and prayer. Of course, you should not lie to your partner. Please also bear in mind that your spouse should not, in all instances, be your counselor. In our opinion, confession to your spouse that would harm or wreck your relationship with him or her may be best kept between you and your Creator—or between you and a counselor, pastor, priest or rabbi—rather than your future husband or wife.

Take the time now to do this important work before moving on to marriage.

Perfect Love

What is the best way to heal past wounds? Healing comes with a bit of education and the awesome power of love. You see, the opposite of love is not hate, as so many think. The opposite of love is fear. To quote Yoda from *Star Wars I: The Phantom Menace*, "Fear is the path to the dark side. Fear leads to anger; anger leads to hate; hate leads to suffering."[1] The Bible teaches us that "perfect love drives out fear" (1 John 4:18).

Regardless of your religious convictions or upbringing, it's most likely that it is love that got you to this point. Your parents, teachers, pastors, coaches, youth group leaders, neighbors and friends were all potential sources of love when you were growing up. Not all may have loved you equally, but the love you were given shaped you in silent and mysterious ways. And any love withheld from you may have yielded deep and detrimental—perhaps unrecognized—wounds.

No matter your past experiences with love, most men and women, before they celebrate their wedding, find it incredibly fun to be in love. It's a time when you are reveling in each other—gazing into each other's eyes, planning your happy life together, exploring the depths of each other's very being. Love is life-giving and holds all possibilities. "Love never fails"—*never* (1 Cor. 13:8).

Did you ever stop to consider that when you are experiencing love, you are experiencing the very essence of God? If you know love, then you already know the most basic and fundamental thing about your Creator. The Bible, God's love letter to us, says, "We know and rely on the love God has for us. God is love. Whoever lives in love lives in God, and God in them" (1 John 4:16).

There is a perfect, unconditional love—what the Bible calls *agape* love. But there are also imperfect, conditional forms of love—*eros* (romantic or erotic love) and *philos* (brotherly love). God's love is perfect, unconditional love; and unconditional love comes only from God. If you and your soul mate love each other unconditionally, then your love for each other is God living in and through you. What a matchless gift!

God's unconditional love is available to each of us who has a personal relationship with God, not only to overflow out of our soul and to those we come in contact with each day, but also to lavish love on our spouse-to-be. This kind of love is the indispensable element for a harmonious and balanced marriage.

The Bible tells us that the fruit of God's Spirit is love, joy, peace, patience, kindness, goodness, faithfulness, gentleness and self-control (see Gal. 5:22-23). I would rather punctuate the verse with a colon after the word "love." The fruit of the spirit is love: joy, peace, patience, etc. In other words, all of the fruit of the Spirit are but manifestations of God's love working in and through us. As Donald Grey Barnhouse wrote:

Joy is love singing,
Peace is love resting,
Patience is love enduring,
Kindness is love's true touch,
Goodness is love's character,
Faithfulness is love's habit,
Gentleness is love's soft side, and
Self-control is love at the steering wheel and, when necessary, touching the brake.[2]

The work you are doing right now is the place to put the power of love to the test. You see, love, God's perfect love, is the most powerful force in the universe—stronger than your sexual past or your marriage's future challenges; stronger than hate, destruction, disaster, disease and even death; stronger than fear.

You may be afraid to face your sexual fears, but it's critical to do so now. You may be afraid to talk to your fiancé about your sexual concerns, but you must. It will take a lot of love to get you through. That's what working on a relationship in the context of engagement and marriage is all about. It's not about avoidance and fear; it's about honesty, perseverance, forgiveness and love.

So this chapter is for you who are sexually experienced. I hope that as you read, you will find answers to your questions, encouragement to face your fears, and peace to replace your worries.

Secondary Virginity

Secondary virginity is the decision of a person who is sexually active to refrain from sexual activity until marriage. If you are currently sexually active, we encourage you and your fiancé to consider putting off any further sexual activity until your wedding night.

Yes, we know that you're in love, and that you've already done "it," so having sex now may not seem like a big deal—but it is!

Here are five reasons to consider secondary virginity during your engagement.

1. Sexual purity before marriage is part of our Creator's divine design. He created us and He created sex. It just makes sense to follow His instructions if we want the happiest, most functional sexual relationship.

2. The Bible suggests that even married couples, at times, may "refrain from sexual intimacy for a limited time, so they can give themselves more completely to prayer" (1 Cor. 7:5, NLT). If even married couples find benefit in separating sexually,

then how much more applicable is this principle to the engagement period, a time in which a couple has the best opportunity to pray for their preparation for marriage?

3. If you do not refrain from sex for a period of time, there is no chance for you to see if your relationship is truly based on a solid foundation of love. Is it just sex or lust? Is it erotic love? Or is it *agape* love? We were created to desire *agape* love and physical companionship. It's part of being human— part of the divine design. However, if you've been sexually active with your future spouse since the beginning of your relationship, how do you know that you are truly in a relationship based on love and not lust? How do you know that you aren't just "in lust"? Give love a chance to prove itself.

4. When you refrain from sex before marriage, there is no possibility of out-of-wedlock pregnancy surprises. No birth control method is as reliable as abstinence. Enough said.

5. Refraining from sex before marriage proves your ability to show self-control and it proves your spouse's as well. When couples are able to prove themselves faithful to each other before marriage, even in the context of control over their sexual behavior with each other, they have a better chance of staying faithful during marriage.

There will be times during your marriage in which one of you will need to refrain from sex: times of separation, medical conditions, pregnancy and aging. All of these conditions can affect your marriage's sexual temperature. We are not animals. We are highly intelligent beings made in the image of God and capable of making sophisticated choices regarding our behavior—even overriding the strong natural urges of sexual activity. Prove yourself worthy of your spouse's trust by showing control over your behavior during your engagement. You will have an entire lifetime together to have sex.

Do you remember the story of Karen in chapter 1? She had already made the mistake of giving in to her fiancé's pressure to have sex during their engagement. As a result, she carried a root of bitterness into her honeymoon. She always wondered, after he had pressured her, if she could really trust him when he was away from her. Rather than making their marriage better, Karen found that premarital sex created a wall between her and Tom.

Men, you can give your fiancé no greater gift than to pledge, along with her, your desire to honor her and your secondary virginity until your wedding night.

The Danger of *Not* Choosing Secondary Virginity

Michael McManus, the cofounder and president of Marriage Savers, writes, "The major thing which men need to do to have a fantastic honeymoon is to remain chaste during the courtship—or at least for several months before the wedding. Consider this: couples who are virgins on the night of their marriage have much lower divorce rates than the sexually active. Below is a table of a study published in the Marriage Savers Mentors' Guide which proves that the sexually active are two-thirds more likely to divorce."[3]

Year Married	Divorce Rate of Those Who Were Virgins When Married	Divorce Rate of Those Who Were *Not* Virgins When Married
1980–1983	14%	24%
1975–1979	21%	34%
1970–1974	30%	46%
1965–1969	30%	50%

McManus adds, "Harriet and I have personally mentored 54 couples. Of that number, only 8 were chaste when they came to us. We asked the other 46 to consider remaining chaste until the wedding, signing an Optional Premarital Sexual Covenant. We showed them this chart and said, 'If you want God's blessing, you need to consider remaining chaste until the wedding. To continue being sexually active will increase your odds of divorce. By remaining chaste from now on, you, in effect, put yourself into the first column.'"[4]

How many of the 46 couples do you think agreed to do so? McManus reveals, "It's over 93 percent; with 43 of the 46 couples agreeing to sign the Optional Sexual Covenant."[5]

Part of the Marriage Savers Premarital Sexual Covenant is for the engaged couple to agree to call their mentor couple if they exceed the level of French kissing. The male must call the male mentor within 24 hours of exceeding the limit, or the female will call the female mentor.

McManus tells about cohabiting couples that he and his wife, Harriet, have mentored who refused to get separate living arrangements, but who did agree to start sleeping in different bedrooms as part of their secondary virginity pledge. One of these couples went to the Caribbean for their honeymoon. When they flew back and landed in Miami to change planes, they called Mike and Harriet to say, "Thank you for giving us a great honeymoon!" McManus adds, "They acted as if we had paid for their honeymoon! In fact, all we had done was make a case for chastity before the wedding."[6]

For Those with Prior Sexual Partners

Great sex, the best sex—within the context of marriage—only works if both partners enter the marriage sexually healthy and maintain sexual health by remaining monogamous (faithful to each other).

If you both are virgins (which we define here as someone who has not had vaginal, anal or oral sex with another), then you can pat yourselves on the back, give each other a high five and skip right over this section to the next. Simply put, you have the best chance for the best and safest sex of all in marriage.

However, if either of you have had a prior sexual partner or other high-risk behaviors for sexually transmitted infections, such as intravenous drug abuse, we need to do a little extra work to get you ready not only for your honeymoon but also for the healthiest marriage possible.

The first step is an in-depth medical examination. Even if your only sexual partner was a former spouse, we still recommend that you have these examinations and tests. Make the medical appointment now. We recommend the following tests well before your wedding day.

For men and women:

- Careful external genital examination, checking especially for genital warts, ulcers or other lesions
- Cultures for gonorrhea and chlamydia
- Culture or test for trichomonas
- Blood tests for HIV (AIDS), syphilis (RPR), hepatitis A, B and C, and herpes viruses

And for women only (sorry, gals, but you've got different parts):

- Pap smear and pelvic examination, with a smear for trichomonas

After you get the results, it is vitally important that you sit down and discuss the findings with your fiancé. Even if you get a clean bill of health, it's important that your future spouse understand your commitment to keep your marriage sexually healthy—relationally, emotionally and physically.

If your testing reveals medical problems, your future spouse has a right to know what he or she is going to be exposed to. This is especially true in the case of viral illnesses such as herpes, HIV and hepatitis. These infections do not yet have a cure and are therefore carried into marriage, potentially putting your spouse's health at risk.

Should you carry one of these illnesses, it is also morally important that you disclose the presence of infection or disease to your fiancé before the marriage. Your fiancé has a right to know what he or she is committing to in marriage, and that certainly includes risking infections with a viral illness.

In addition, having a discussion regarding viral illnesses in the context of your future marriage relationship gives both of you an opportunity to come to terms with the problem and form a plan for addressing it in your sexual relationship. If one or both of you has a positive test for a sexually transmitted infection, we believe that you should both be counseled *together* by a medical doctor *and* a faith-sensitive counselor. It's critical to clear up any and all misperceptions, emotional baggage or responses, and potential roots of bitterness or anger.

For a Virgin Whose Fiancé Has Had a Prior Sexual Partner

For those of you preparing for marriage with a fiancé who has had a former sexual partner (or maybe even several sexual partners) outside of a previous marriage relationship, we'd like to take a moment to discuss forgiveness.

We simply do not recommend entering into a marriage agreement with someone who (1) has shown himself or herself incapable of being sexually loyal or monogamous, (2) is not willing to commit to being sexually pure from now until your wedding day, and (3) is not willing to vow to God, you, your parents and your witnesses on your wedding day that he or she will be faithful *only* to you until death. Anything else is a recipe for heartache and disaster.

Without question, in-depth, faith-based counseling will be helpful. But if after counseling, your fiancé is unwilling to make an unconditional vow to remain faithful to you until you die, then you must carefully consider cutting your losses now, before the wedding, and save yourself the potential future cost of divorce court and worse.

Are you now engaged to a fiancé who was unfaithful to his or her previous spouse? Perhaps you were even the one with whom your fiancé chose to cheat. If so, and this is not dealt with now, there may well come another woman (or man) into your marriage.

When Rebecca married Jerry, she knew that he had been involved in several relationships with other women. At first, she thought this was great. "After all," she explained to me, "he's sexually experienced. He says I'll be learning from the very best!"

However, his history and their relationship sent up red flags for me. One flag was that Jerry had admitted to having two affairs while in a past marriage. The other was when Rebecca confided to me, "He says that he can't wait to show me some pornographic videos to help out our sex life."

I had a talk with Rebecca and presented her with the same principles you are now reading. She heard what I was saying but could not bring herself to confront Jerry about his past behavior. She tried to reassure me. "He swears to me that it is all in the past!"

When I learned that Rebecca refused to confront him, I offered to help. "Why don't you *and* Jerry come in for an appointment?" Rebecca said she'd think about it, but I never saw her again until about two years after her wedding. She came in for symptoms of severe depression. Her marriage was ending—all of her dreams shattered into a thousand pieces. Although Jerry had remained faithful for a year or so, she was devastated when she discovered he was addicted to Internet pornography and she also discovered that he was in an affair with a married woman.

If your fiancé refuses to deal with his or her past sexual misadventures and refuses to completely commit to being sexually faithful to you and pure with you, then be prepared to be the heartbroken spouse down the line.

What do we recommend? Run! Now!! And don't look back.

If, however, your future spouse has had a sexual past outside of marriage, regrets those actions in the context of now preparing for a lifetime commitment to you and has not only asked for your forgiveness but is also promising and committing to be sexually pure from now until death do you part, then we still seriously encourage caution and recommend that you *both* get some faith-based and spiritually sensitive counseling together *before* your wedding.

In addition, there's another critical step for you: forgiving *and* forgetting. Will this be hard to do? Nope. It will be impossible! At least in the flesh.

However, add love and not only will forgiveness and forgetting become possible but they will also be promising and fruitful. Forgiveness has been described as one of the 10 essentials of highly healthy people.[7]

One of my homework assignments for you is to obtain the book *God's Design for the Highly Healthy Person* and study the chapter on forgiveness (chapter 4, "Practice Acceptance and Letting Go, The Essential of Forgiveness").[8] In that chapter, there is a necessary nine-step process for forgiving *and* forgetting.

To forgive and forget will be an impossible process without *agape* love. So often we think of love in the romantic, mushy sense, but this is where real love has its chance to shine. The Bible teaches that real love is patient, kind, not jealous or boastful, proud or rude. Real love doesn't demand its own way, is not irritable, and keeps no record when it has been wronged (see 1 Cor. 13:4-5).

Forgiving and forgetting is even more important if there are medical, spiritual or emotional consequences to prior actions that your fiancé is working through in preparation for marriage to you.

Handle it with *agape* love; only God's love in you can equip, empower and enable you to forgive *and* forget. Allow your fiancé to work through his or her issues and accept the changes as he or she works with you toward putting the past behind.

Work overtime to avoid carrying grudges, anger, bitterness or unforgiveness into your marriage. These attitudes can kill you and your marriage. Commit to never bring up what is past—ever. This is a time for new beginnings and healing. Not forgiving a truly repentant fiancé is like trying to hurt him or her by slowly sipping on cyanide. Understand that the forgiveness process is not just a nice add-on to marriage; it is *critical* for a successful marriage and spiritual life. After all, our Father in heaven offers to forgive *and* forget *all* our sins. And Jesus commands us to forgive others as we desire to be forgiven (see Matt. 6:14).

When Both of You Have Had Prior Sexual Partners

It is critical that the two of you spend time discussing sexual purity and secondary virginity from now until you are married. Then it's vital to set a date—make it as soon as possible—to immediately cease intimate sexual activity until marriage.

This pact is an essential step in which you demonstrate to one another that you can and will be sexually pure before marriage. If your fiancé cannot control his or her sexual urges and temptations before marriage, we can virtually guarantee that he or she will *not* be able to do so after marriage. Period.

We simply do not recommend entering into marriage with someone who tells you that he or she is incapable of being sexually loyal or monogamous to you both before and after your wedding. It's a recipe for heartache and disaster.

As we told you earlier, couples who are virgins (or secondary virgins) on the night of their marriage have much lower divorce rates than the sexually active. If you want God's blessing, you need to consider remaining chaste until the wedding. To continue being sexually active will increase your odds of divorce.

You both deserve to know that your spouse-to-be will be loyal to you. And your fiancé deserves to know that you will be loyal to him or her. If either of you is not willing to make a commitment to sexual purity from now until you are married, then you are far less likely, in our opinion, to have a healthful marriage. Your risk of being unfaithful or having an unfaithful spouse during your marriage soars if one or both of you cannot be sexually pure before your wedding.

Your Sexual Fears

Sex is great. It is divinely designed to be that way. Sex in the context of a loving, committed marriage is the most satisfying sex on the planet.

In order to experience the divine design for a great sex life in your marriage, take the time now and prepare yourself spiritually and emotionally for your honeymoon and your marriage. The biblical design is for you to have a marriage that is ruled by love, not fear, and that goes double for your sex life! Sex was created specifically to remain within the context of marriage and to be initiated in a honeymoon that has the potential to last a lifetime—full of pleasure and satisfaction, with love as the guiding emotion.

Make a decision now to choose to face your fears about your sexual concerns and replace fear with confidence and love.

For Thought and Prayer

1. Some of the discussion in this chapter may have helped you identify important sexual baggage—issues that you need to work through well before your honeymoon. Take a moment and write down specific areas you may need to work on and how you might go about that important work during your engagement.

2. If you have especially challenging issues in your past regarding sex, such as rape, abuse, extreme promiscuity or sexual identity crisis, and have not sought appropriate therapy with a spiritually sensitive, licensed psychologist, pastoral professional or psychiatrist, we urge you to make an appointment today.

3. If necessary, are you willing to consider deferring your wedding and honeymoon plans until such time that you are emotionally, relationally *and* spiritually prepared to go forward in a healthy marriage relationship?

4. Do you feel that it is important and safe to share with your fiancé any significant emotional challenges concerning this area of your life?

5. Are you committed to healing any hurts before going forward in marriage?

6. Do you believe that when discussed in the context of a healthy, loving relationship, working through these issues builds trust?

7. Is it possible that your future partner may also choose to participate in the counseling process and this may have significant benefit to your future together?

8. How and when do you plan to implement each of these decisions and practice what you believe?

Resources

Kendall, R. T. *Total Forgiveness.* Lake Mary, FL: Charisma House, 2002.

Larimore, Walt. *God's Design for the Highly Healthy Person.* Grand Rapids, MI: Zondervan Publishing House, 2004.

Chapter Six

A HEALTHY
HONEYMOON

It is not the healthy who need a doctor, but the sick.

LUKE 5:31

My son, Scott, and his new wife, Jennifer, both wanted a honeymoon that was divine. They wanted plenty of rest, simplicity in travel and arrangements, a dreamy condominium, and activities they both could enjoy. But to have the honeymoon of a lifetime—one that would be the foundation of an until-death-do-us-part marriage—they knew that this type of healthful honeymoon needed to be planned.

So far, we've discussed the "sexy" stuff. Now, let's get down to some of the more mundane yet still critical issues surrounding the planning of the honeymoon of a lifetime.

The Definition of Health

Our modern word "health" is said to be derived from an old English word that means "whole." In other words, being healthy means being whole. I like to say that being healthy means that our whole being must be whole. This wholeness requires a balance between four unique spheres of health.

The physician Luke's writing in the Bible includes these words: "Jesus grew in wisdom and stature, and in favor with God and men" (Luke 2:52, *NIV*). In other words, Jesus had to be healthy emotionally and mentally (in wisdom), physically (in stature), relationally (in favor with men) and spiritually (in favor with God).

Nearly 2,000 years later, in 1948, the World Health Organization recognized these four spheres of health when they defined health this way:

> Health is a state of complete physical, mental, social and spiritual well-being and not merely the absence of disease or infirmity. The enjoyment of the highest attainable standard of health is one of the fundamental rights of every human being without distinction of race, religion, political belief, economic, or social condition.[1]

A physician friend of mine once told me, "[Unlike the WHO definition of health,] I think that true health involves our entire beings. The physical, mental, and spiritual elements must all be functioning as God designed them to function if we are to be truly healthy. The physical may actually be the most unimportant of the three, because with good mental and spiritual health we can still be content, even though our bodies may be unhealthy."[2]

In *The Bible and Healing*, John Wilkinson, a British physician who was both a medical missionary and a biblical scholar, said that while the Bible appears to say little about health as defined in strictly medical or mental terms, "human wholeness or health is the main topic of the Bible. . . . It is only when human beings are whole and their relationships right, that they can be described as truly healthy."[3]

In my book *God's Design for the Highly Healthy Person*, I wrote:

> I have come to believe that being healthy—truly healthy—is not dependent on physical well-being alone. Being highly healthy means being healthy in every area of your life during every stage of your life. It means being balanced in these areas: body, mind, spirit, and community—what I call the four "wheels" of health. By balancing these aspects of health, you can become blessed and, thus, highly healthy.[4]

Healthful Honeymoon

A highly healthy honeymoon—one that is healthful—must balance physical, emotional, relational *and* spiritual health. Unless these four "marriage wheels" are balanced and inflated, then your ride down the road of marriage may be bumpy indeed and you may even be in for a flat tire along the way.

That's why we've spent so much time in this book talking about the spiritual, relational and emotional aspects of marriage that form the foundation of a healthy honeymoon. There are also a number of physical health aspects to address.

Preparation for a Physically Healthful Honeymoon

We hope neither you nor your spouse will be in need of a physician during your honeymoon. To that end, some of what we'll discuss here will help you prevent physical illness during your first week or two together as a married couple.

You'll also find yourself better prepared for minor medical conditions and able to take care of them yourselves without the hassle of seeking inconvenient or expensive medical care while away. We'll also help you identify when you need to go beyond self-treatment and seek outside medical care.

Since we've already dealt with the sexual health issues (physical, emotional, relational and spiritual), let's turn our attention to some basic information for travel and general medical health, along with resources for identifying preparations or medical needs specific to your physical health and your honeymoon destination.

State Requirements for Health Testing for Marriage License

Some states still require that blood be drawn to test for sexually transmitted infections or genetic disorders before the issue of a marriage license. If you live in one of these states, it is very important that you comply with

plenty of time to get the results back before the wedding. We recommend doing this at least one month or more before the wedding.

States that require blood tests:

- Connecticut
- District of Columbia (Washington, DC)
- Indiana
- Mississippi
- Montana[5]

General Travel Readiness

How would you rate your general physical health today? Do you eat
healthily? Do you exercise? Do you manage stress well? Do you get
enough sleep? Do you take your vitamins and other medications as
prescribed? Do you make (and keep) your doctors' appointments?
How physically healthy would you like to be by the time you go on
your honeymoon?

Bride-to-be, you are at risk for using extreme weight-loss plans and
not using good stress management. Thin at what price? You do not
want to enter your first week of marriage squeezed into that teeny-
waisted wedding gown, weak from poor nutrition, exhausted from the
stress, and fainting from lack of oxygen! That's no way to enjoy your
new husband!

Jenny, a patient of mine, is an example of this behavior. She was a
bit overweight before her wedding. Rather than talk to me about a
slow, steady and healthy increase in exercise combined with a healthy
nutritional plan and plenty of refreshing rest and recreation, she followed the advice of her brother: He was a high school wrestler and had
her follow a regimen of unhealthy fasting, the ingestion of potentially
dangerous supplements and doing too much exercise in too short a
period of time.

By Jenny's wedding day, she had lost the weight she wanted to lose
but was frail, tremulous and pale. Makeup made up for her pallor, but
her body could not accommodate her compromised health. To the

horror of everyone at her wedding, she fainted at the altar and could not be quickly revived. An ambulance was called, and after intravenous fluids, the shaken bride was able to return to and complete her wedding ceremony a few hours later. But she could not attend her reception and had to delay the honeymoon.

Men, you may not have the same reputation for extreme weight-loss schemes leading up to the wedding, but we've seen more than our share of men suffering from unhealthy activities—overeating, under-exercising, smoking, poor stress management. And most men are not as wise as the woman they are marrying in seeking preventive health care.

For example, the average woman consults a doctor 150 percent more frequently than does the average man and is significantly more likely to keep up with her annual medical visits.[6] The cost? Guys are significantly under-diagnosed for medical conditions such as high blood pressure, depression or diabetes—any of which can greatly affect honeymoon activities, not to mention marital and life expectancy!

Picture instead yourself and your spouse *physically* healthy, vivacious *and* vibrant on your honeymoon—tired maybe from the wedding planning and activities (and honeymoon activities) but healthy, strong and able to fully take pleasure in your new roles as husband and wife—emotionally, relationally and spiritually intact and growing.

How can you best get there? Begin today!

Healthy Lifestyle During Your Engagement

Choose to live a healthy lifestyle during your engagement—practicing good nutrition, and getting adequate sleep and regular exercise.

You may want to pick up a copy of my book *God's Design for the Highly Healthy Person.*[7] At the start of the book is an assessment tool to self-rate your physical, emotional, relational and spiritual health. The book also includes an in-depth Relationship Questionnaire and a detailed Spiritual Life Profile that you and your fiancé can use to evaluate your health and wholeness.

You can also access my *Assess Your Health Assessment Tool* at www.DrWalt.com.

If You Choose to Lose Weight, Do So Wisely

Sue is a Weight Watchers lifetime graduate. After delivery of her fourth child in six years (Sue says, "Okay, maybe not the most healthy choice"), she found herself 65 pounds over her ideal body weight. One of the most challenging things she's ever done was to lose that weight. She did it with the help of Weight Watchers—and she has kept it off.

We both highly recommend Weight Watchers (www.weightwatchers .com) for these reasons:

- Weight Watchers recommends dietary suggestions that are medically and nutritionally sound. The program teaches you how to eat healthily instead of handing you prepackaged meals.
- Weight Watchers recommends a reasonable exercise plan.
- Weight Watchers uses important tools for modifying behavior— education, accountability, a support group and a way to journal.
- Weight Watchers is affordably priced.
- Weight Watchers teaches and encourages lifelong health habits, not just how to lose weight.
- Weight Watchers is highly accessible and has local meetings in virtually every community in the United States. Still can't make it? Log on to www.weightwatchers.com for an online version with great tools for managing your diet and health.
- Weight Watchers has a system that is clinically proven. If you follow it, it works.

Get a Premarital Preventive Medical Examination

I was pleased that both Scott and Jennifer had preventive examinations during their engagement. In Scott's case, his primary care physician discovered a blood pressure problem that has a deep root in my wife's family. Undiagnosed hypertension can lead to a bevy of medical problems (such as heart disease, heart attack or stroke) that can be prevented with early recognition and treatment. Without this examination, it's likely that Scott may have gone many more years without recognizing this problem.

Make an appointment to visit your primary care physician (family physician, internist or obstetrician/gynecologist) and get a thorough general physical examination, especially if it has been more than a year since your last one.

Talk to your doctor about your general medical health, any concerns you might have and your plans for travel. (See destination-specific concerns and sexual health concerns sections for more topics to discuss at your visit.)

Make sure that you fill your prescriptions and pack medications with you when you travel. Also ask your doctor for a written prescription for each medicine you routinely take and have it with you on the trip. Your doctor can help you get fine-tuned and in shape for your honeymoon.

Stop Smoking or Using Tobacco Products

If you are a smoker or use tobacco products daily, we don't have to tell you how addictive they are. And you know as well as we do all of the reasons to stop—not the least of which is a longer life, a healthier life and healthier children when they come along.

What you may not know is that people who choose to stop smoking before their wedding (or before the birth of a child) are much more likely not only to stop successfully but also not as likely to fall back to tobacco use at a later time.

If you or your fiancé use tobacco products, there is no better time to stop than now. If you have any trouble, discuss this with your pharmacist or physician, who can be of great help to you.

Commit to Getting Enough Sleep During Your Engagement

This is especially true the week of the wedding. One wise future husband made his bride-to-be a promise to get at least 8 hours of sleep a night the week of the wedding—instead of his usual 5 hours of sleep per night—which left him groggy most of the day. Was she ever grateful!

Study the Ethical Concerns Regarding Birth Control Methods

In our experience, the choice of whether or not to use birth control, and a couple's choice of the type of birth control, is an intensely personal decision fraught with emotional, moral and ethical consideration. When it comes to hormonal birth control, there is a debate among deeply pro-life, Christian physicians about whether hormonal birth control sometimes works by an abortifacient effect.

In other words, some physicians and researchers believe that hormonal birth control may, at times, cause an embryo *not* to implant in the uterus (the womb). If you believe, as we do, that life begins at conception (fertilization), then anything that unnaturally ends that life, before birth, would be an abortifacient (cause an abortion).

I believe this risk is possible, while Sue thinks it is unlikely.[8] Nevertheless, because this debate is so *very* complex and the ultimate decision you make, as a couple, will be deeply reflective of your religious and moral views and will also be influenced by your physical health and mutual desire for children, we cannot hope to begin to offer appropriate individual counsel in the format of this book.

Rather, we encourage you to study this controversy together and discuss birth control with your pastor, priest or rabbi, as well as your mentor couple and personal physician.[9]

Talk About Your Physical Health Expectations

Take some time to sit down and talk with each other about your health expectations for each other in marriage. Think about how you want to encourage and care for each other.

Most engaged couples take for granted that they will live together (and sleep together) as a married couple. Many underestimate the impact that a married couple has on each other's health habits.

Start your marriage off on the right foot, during your honeymoon, with good married health habits. Eat healthy meals together. Exercise together. Stop bad habits (such as smoking) together. Encourage each other to keep physically healthy for a lifelong healthy marriage.

Consider Menstrual Manipulation or Menstrual Shifting

One recent advance in hormonal birth control medicines is the development of continuous dosing birth control pills. Rather than having a period every month, women using this medication have a period every three months (only four periods a year), thus reducing any problems that may be aggravated by monthly cycling, such as premenstrual syndrome (PMS), dysmenorrhea (painful menses), fibroids, abnormal or heavy menstrual bleeding, or pelvic pain. In addition to daily oral pills, continuous dosing methods also include injectable, implantable, patch and vaginal ring devices.

Not only can these medications be used to stop periods for these reasons, but they may also be used to safely prevent menstruation at inconvenient times, such as during your wedding and honeymoon. Talk to your doctor about continuous dosing of contraceptive medication when you go for your pre-wedding checkup.

Another technique we have recommended for honeymoon couples is menstrual shifting. Instead of stopping periods completely, this technique just shifts the period for a week or two so that it does not coincide with the wedding. This technique requires about 6 months advance planning to adjust the body to the new cycles without breakthrough bleeding problems; so if the wedding is closer than that, please don't start trying to shift things around now.

In order to find out when your period is due, use the menstrual calendar in appendix E. Look at your last six cycles, calculate your average cycle length by counting the number of days from the beginning of one menses to the beginning of the next.

A normal menstrual cycle length is 26 to 35 days. If you are taking regular cycling birth control pills, your cycle length is 28 days. Using your average cycle length and the first day of your last menstrual period, mark your predicted menstrual cycles for the months leading up to your wedding. In order to shift a period, it is far easier to shorten a cycle length (make a period start early) than it is to lengthen it (make it start later).

Using birth control pills, your doctor can help you schedule shortened cycles to adjust your period to fall just before your wedding. Prepare at least six months in advance, if you wish to shift the date of your period to not coincide with your wedding date or honeymoon.

Update Your Immunizations

In general, you both should be current on the following immunizations, recommended for all adults, whether you are traveling or not, by the Centers for Disease Control and Prevention (CDC). You can find more detailed information at the CDC website.[10]

- Diphtheria, tetanus, and acellular pertussis (DTaP)
- Measles, mumps, rubella (MMR)
- Varicella (chickenpox)
- Hepatitis A and B
- Meningitis

If you have additional risk factors for disease based on your lifestyle, work environment, medical conditions or otherwise, you may also need to be vaccinated with the following:

- Influenza (usually only given October through December of each year)
- Pneumococcal

Gather First-Aid Items for Your Honeymoon Kit

Whether you're planning a simple honeymoon close to home or an exotic one overseas, there are some general first-aid measures that any traveler should consider bringing in a travel kit. A convenient list of products to purchase and bring with you whenever you travel is provided in appendix B.

Pain Relievers

Probably one of the last things a husband wants to hear on a honeymoon is, "Not tonight, honey. I have a headache." From headaches to vaginitis, from sore muscles to sprained ankles, nothing is more essential in your first-aid kit for travel than your favorite pain reliever. We're partial to ibuprofen, but people with sensitive stomachs should probably stick to acetaminophen (Tylenol).

Upset Stomach Relief

Travel brings with it exposure to new foods and bacterial environments. We personally recommend taking along loperamide (Imodium AD), a potent intestinal antispasmodic for diarrhea and cramping relief. If you have a sensitive stomach, packing an antacid such as Maalox or Mylanta in tablet form may help you avoid an unpleasant episode. For acid indigestion or heartburn, consider packing over-the-counter preparations such as cimetidine (Tagamet), ranitidine (Zantac), famotidine (Pepcid) or omeprazole (Prilosec).

We also rarely travel out of the country without a filled prescription for metronidazole (Flagyl) or ciprofloxacin (Cipro). On a honeymoon, this antibiotic can be helpful for treating intestinal disturbances due to bacteria or parasites. It also happens to be a treatment of choice for bacterial vaginosis, an overgrowth of normal vaginal bacteria. *One word of caution when taking Flagyl:* Don't drink alcohol, as it can make you very sick to your stomach.

Pepto-Bismol, in doses of two 262-milligram tablets four times a day, has been shown to prevent traveler's diarrhea.

Rifaximin, a fairly new antibiotic, is being touted by some travel doctors as a safe and effective treatment in most patients with traveler's diarrhea—and even to prevent traveler's diarrhea. In our opinion, it offers no advantages over Cipro or Flagyl and is less convenient to take.

Talk to your doctor to determine which prescription antibiotics (if any) you should fill before heading off into the sunset.

Multivitamins

This is just good general, daily advice. Take a multivitamin. Eat healthy and get plenty of rest. When traveling, it is especially important to make sure you get the right balance of nutrients. Be sure that your multivitamin contains at least 50 micrograms of folic acid per dose. For women, taking enough folic acid when you are *not* pregnant helps to dramatically reduce your baby's risk of spinal defects when you *do* become pregnant.

Cold Relief

A runny nose just isn't sexy! Pack some pseudoephedrine (Sudafed), unless your doctor has told you that you can't take it. In most states, this is available without a prescription, but it will be located behind the counter in your pharmacy. You'll need to ask the pharmacist for it. If you have allergies, don't forget a nonsedating antihistamine, such as over-the-counter loratadine (Claritin). Also, a nasal spray decongestant, such as Afrin Nasal Spray, is a very effective decongestant but should not be used longer than five days. Beyond that, pack your favorite cold, cough or upper respiratory infection medications, just in case.

Band-Aids and Moleskin
You never know when you'll need a bandage or get a blister. Purchase a small box with several sizes of Band-Aids.

Topicals
For the relief of insect bites, topical irritations and minor allergic reactions, I recommend 1% hydrocortisone cream. Antibiotic ointments, such as over-the-counter Neosporin or Bacitracin or the prescription Bactroban, are helpful in the treatment of minor cuts and scrapes.

Seasickness Patches
If you plan to ride in a boat, don't forget your prescription for scopolamine patches or over-the-counter Dramamine tablets. If you purchase the patches, read the instructions very carefully, and be absolutely sure to wash your hands after handling the patch.

Altitude Sickness
Talk to your physician about taking a prescription, such as acetazolamide (Diamox) or dexamethasone, if you are going to high altitudes (above 9,500 feet), particularly if you will not have time to acclimate (go up in altitude slowly) or have a history of altitude sickness. These medications can be used to help prevent or treat high altitude sickness.

Other Prescriptions
Complete your Honeymoon Kit by throwing in your other daily prescriptions and medications—both his and hers. Include extras of medications that you may take only on an as-needed basis. Also be sure to get a separate written prescription for *each* medication you take and

keep the written prescriptions in a separate bag. There are two reasons for this: (1) to refill your prescriptions in case they are lost or stolen, and (2) for international travel, to document that your medications are legal and legitimate.

Destination-Specific Concerns

Depending on your honeymoon destination, many foreign destinations require additional immunization or medical coverage. For instance, when traveling to countries where malaria is prevalent, prevention with any of several medications is recommended. For a complete list of vaccinations and travel recommendations, particularly for foreign travel, check out the CDC's travel website at www.cdc.gov/travel/.

Travel Health Online's website, at www.tripprep.com, is a comprehensive medical site for travel, which also includes specific information regarding health providers for the area in which you are traveling. Write down the name of the doctor or clinic that you would use in case of an emergency on your trip.

It's also important to consider special circumstances that may affect your honeymoon travel. Please consider the following conditions in making your plans. More information for these and other travel advisories may also be found at Travel Health Online:

- Altitude sickness
- Malaria prevention
- Seasickness
- Water and diving safety
- Pregnancy—yes, we know, ideally this may not be how you would plan on going into a marriage, but realistically, we know that some of you will be pregnant already on your honeymoon. A few more of you may actually become so on your honeymoon! Please make sure you check with your doctor regarding recommendations for air travel and other activities that may affect pregnancy. And don't forget to bring along those prenatal vitamins!

- Jet lag
- Sun and heat safety

Conclusion

Whether you are planning a honeymoon close to home or a more ambitious foreign trip, we want you to be physically healthy before and during your trip. Even beyond that, part of having a long and happy marriage is taking good care of that earth-suit the Creator gave each of us! If you are not already making healthy daily choices, we encourage you to begin today. That's the best way we know to help you have the healthiest honeymoon (and marriage) for a lifetime.

For Thought and Prayer

1. What habits for physical health do you personally want to take into your engagement? Take a moment and write down your health goals for the next several months.

2. What habits for physical health do you and your fiancé want to take into your marriage? Talk these over together and take some time to record your health goals as a couple for your marriage.

3. What health habits could you share with each other now and in your marriage? Eating healthy meals together? Exercising together? Breaking bad health habits such as smoking?

4. How and when do you plan to implement each of these decisions?

Resources

Centers for Disease Control and Prevention. www.cdc.gov/travel and www.cdc.gov/nip/recs/adult-schedule.pdf.

Larimore, Walt. *God's Design for the Highly Healthy Person.* Grand Rapids, MI: Zondervan Publishing House, 2004.

Travel Health Online. www.tripprep.com.

Weight Watchers. www.weightwatchers.com.

Chapter Seven

HONEYMOON TRAVEL CONCERNS

*Don't lose sight of good planning and insight. They keep you safe on
your way and keep your feet from stumbling.*

PROVERBS 3:21,23, *NLT*

The Value of Planning Ahead

Whenever Sue has a surgical case scheduled, she finds herself
going over the planned operation in her head the night before,
often step by step, visualizing every movement of the procedure and
every possible complication. She carefully considers the individual
patient and her unique problem. She thinks ahead about what instru-
ments, sutures and surgical approach to use, what the surgical field
will look like and what defines a successful outcome. She thinks about
how her patient will react with the result of her surgery and how this
procedure will be better than any like it that she's done before.

This ritual of planning is trained into a doctor during his or her
residency. Even though Sue's training was over a decade ago, she still
uses this mental planning. It has served her well in the operating room.

If you think of the times when you've looked into the cockpit of an
airplane when you boarded the plane, what did you see? The pilots
going through a step-by-step checklist to check that they have everything they need and that everything they need is in proper working
condition.

What Sue does before entering the operating room and what your
pilot does before takeoff serves them both well. And the same process
can serve you just as well in preparing to take off for your honeymoon.

The tradition of the honeymoon dates back several centuries as a time when newlyweds sequestered themselves away from the rest of the world to revel in the joy of their fresh-from-the-altar marital bliss. Regardless of your choice of travel destination or budget, this can be an incredibly special time for you as a couple. It's a time for new beginnings and new experiences with each other as husband and wife.

It's a time most couples look forward to as a period of rest—and well they should! After the hustle and bustle of weeks of planning for the wedding, the whirlwind of the wedding day itself and the wedding night, it's no wonder most couples just want rest!

A little bit of careful planning and preparation will ensure that you have the most worry-free honeymoon possible. Remember, the focus should not be on how exotic the destination is, how extravagant the vacation package, or how packed you can make the itinerary. The focus should be on you, as a couple, getting started out on the right foot in your marriage.

As you continue planning your honeymoon of a lifetime, take advantage of the calendar, the checklists, the pocket pages and worksheets provided in the appendices to record your honeymoon plans and to help keep your documents organized and close at hand.

Before we get to the mechanics of the honeymoon, let's talk a bit about the timing.

Sheva Brachot

We find that most couples leave from the wedding and depart on their honeymoon that day or the next. Not only may that not be the wisest choice, but it is not even a time-tested or traditional preference.

Talking about those who leave immediately on their honeymoon, film critic and talk-radio host Michael Medved says, "Consider the underlying message this sends. After what is usually a very public ceremony, they abruptly escape from the very community that helped them consecrate their vows."[1]

Mr. Medved reminds Christians of the ancient wedding tradition of waiting several days or a week before the honeymoon. He writes about the Jewish tradition called *sheva brachot* or the Seven Blessings, wherein the newlywed couple stays at the home of a different family every night for several nights.[2] Traditionally, the families with whom the newlyweds stay are from the same faith community and have stable, successful marriages.

Medved calls this "a movable feast of sorts" and "just plain fun." Furthermore, he believes "this tradition places the marriage in the context of a larger community." He points out that "each evening an additional two guests the newlyweds don't know are invited to celebrate with them, expanding the circle of friends and broadening the context of the marriage."[3]

"Therefore," Medved says, "the Seven Blessings is for the community's benefit as much as the newlyweds." He adds, "If you enter into a marriage knowing your relationship means something to other people, you won't be so quick to say, 'I don't want this any more,' and walk out. There would be an element of embarrassment, an embarrassment of consequences beyond yourself."[4]

Could this ancient Jewish tradition be used by Christians? Medved answers, "Frankly, it's always surprised me that it hasn't become more widespread in the evangelical community." The form and format of this tradition isn't nearly as important, according to Medved, as the message: "What really matters is that they communicate that the success of the new marriage matters to them."[5]

Rest, Rest, Rest

I was privileged to have a grandfather who understood another tradition. He counseled me that after my wedding, I should wait several days before leaving on my honeymoon. He taught me that the primary reason for doing this was just to rest. And indeed, through the years, I've seen scores of couples spend thousands upon thousands of dollars to arrive at a swank resort in a fun vacation area just to sleep in utter exhaustion for several days.

Men, it's especially important for you to understand the physical and emotional toll the wedding ceremony will take on your new bride. She will most likely be exhausted on her wedding night and for at least another day or two. Why not consider resting a few days before leaving—for both your and her benefit?

Barb and I were married in Baton Rouge, Louisiana, the town in which we were going to live as newlyweds. So we chose to spend our first few days of marriage in our first apartment. No one knew but Barb's mom. Keeping this secret from the wedding party, we thought, would protect us from unforeseen pranks. As I was to learn, there was much more value to this choice than just giving us a few days to rest.

Guys, for many (if not most) women, their home is their nest—their comfort zone, their physical sanctuary, their emotional refuge, their spiritual harbor. Therefore, for many women, having their first sexual encounter with their new husband in their own bed with their own sheets and their own pillow can be incredibly special and fulfilling.

To wake up the morning after the wedding near her own bathroom and her own kitchen (and in the case of Barb, near her own coffee maker and her special coffees), can give a woman great security and comfort.

After a few days of much-needed rest and some incredibly meaningful meals and time with our parents and immediate family, we left on a wonderful honeymoon that we deeply enjoyed.

Barb and I have suggested this tradition to the couples for whom we provide premarital counseling. Each couple has adopted the tradition to fit their circumstances.

Tom and Jennifer were married in her hometown and in her family's church. After the wedding, they flew *not* to their honeymoon destination but to their newly set-up apartment in the town in which they were going to live. The first few days of their honeymoon were in their new apartment, and they shared dinner with a mentor couple the night before flying out for their honeymoon a few days later.

Lisa and Mike spent their first night in their apartment and then, in compliance with an old family tradition, had the immediate family over the next day to share memories, pictures, laughter, and to open wedding presents. They left for their honeymoon rested and satisfied a couple of days later.

Other couples, for financial and stewardship reasons, will spend their first days of marital bliss in their new apartment or home and save their honeymoon for a special holiday or seasonal time later that year. The possible timing options are as numerous and varied as are newlywed couples. But these old traditions are, in our opinion, worthy of resurrection and serious consideration.

Whether your first days are spent on the road or under your own roof, there are a number of items to consider as you wisely prepare for your honeymoon, and we'll examine a few of these now. Above all, don't just plan a fancy vacation. You have the rest of your lives to go on fancy vacations. We challenge you to look beyond this week as a week of vacation and focus your honeymoon plans on the goal of setting a foundation for a lifetime of happiness together.

Sleep, Blessed Sleep

Aldous Huxley famously wrote, "That we are not much sicker and much madder than we are is due exclusively to that most blessed and blessing of all natural graces, sleep." Sleep is a basic necessity of life and is as important to our health and wellbeing as air, food and water. When we get a good night's sleep, we wake up feeling refreshed, alert and ready to face the challenges of the day. With refreshing sleep, we're more alert, less moody, perform better and are generally happier.

When we don't get a good night's sleep, every part of our lives can suffer. So, revitalizing nights of sleep before the wedding—especially the night before your wedding—are critical.

Here are some hints to be sure you will sleep well in the weeks and days before your honeymoon:

- Avoid all alcohol, as it almost always leads to disrupted sleep.
- Avoid caffeine (coffee, tea, soft drinks, chocolate) after 3 P.M.
- Exercise regularly and daily, but complete your workout at least three hours before bedtime.
- Establish a regular relaxing, non-alerting, bedtime routine (e.g., taking a bath or relaxing in a hot tub).
- Avoid television an hour before bedtime.

- Create a sleep-conducive environment that is dark, quiet and preferably cool and comfortable.
- Try to get 8 to 9 hours of sleep each night.

Even if you follow all this advice, there will still be some situations in which a mild sleeping pill may help you obtain a long and restful night's sleep, such as the night or two before your wedding, while flying overnight (if you choose a honeymoon location overseas) or the first few nights of your honeymoon.

You may have heard stories about the horrible side effects of sleeping pills or tales of brides or grooms sleeping late or dozing off at the altar because they took them. But almost all of those stories occurred with the older sleep agents. The newer sleeping pills are designed to help you fall asleep quickly and wake up refreshed. The three drugs now recommended as the first-choice medications for short-term insomnia are zolpidem (Ambien, Ambien CR), zaleplon (Sonata) and eszopiclone (Lunesta).

If you decide to have a few sleeping pills on hand, I recommend you talk to your doctor about getting a prescription with just a few tablets (or, better yet, some free samples if the doctor has them) and give them a try a couple of months before your honeymoon. That way you'll know how your body responds to the particular medication. Even if you don't need them, it can be comforting to have them on standby, just in case.

The Old Testament prophet Jeremiah described waking from a refreshing night's sleep. When he awoke, he said, "My sleep had been pleasant to me" (Jer. 31:26). May yours, before and during your honeymoon, be pleasant as well.

Preventing Jet Lag

If you are planning to travel across several time zones to get to your honeymoon destination—and especially if you'll be flying overnight—you will need to prepare for jet lag. The shift in time and light forces your brain and body to alter from its normal wake-sleep pattern and adjust to the new time zone.

All of the tips on the travel websites and in the travel books (e.g., trying to shift your sleep and wake times gradually to the new schedule and adopt the sleep-wake cycle of your destination, changing your diet, changing your exercise habits) simply do not seem to work for my patients during the week prior to their honeymoon. Over-the-counter medications, such as antihistamines and melatonin, may not be dependable and may even have side effects. So, what have I found to be most effective?

Glad you asked! Studies show—and my patients testify—that using a mild prescription sleep medication for two to three nights before you travel on the plane, while flying overnight, and then for two to three nights at your honeymoon destination resets you body's wake-sleep cycle while providing refreshing sleep. For the trip back, you just reverse the process. However, you must be sure to obtain and try the prescription several weeks before you travel to see how you respond to it.

So, whether the first days of your marriage are spent on the road, overseas or under your own roof, there are a number of items to consider as you wisely prepare for your honeymoon, and we'll examine a few of these now. Above all, don't just plan a fancy vacation. You have the rest of your lives to go on fancy vacations. We challenge you to look beyond this week as a week of vacation and focus your honeymoon plans on the goal of setting a foundation for a lifetime of happiness together.

Simplicity

Melanie had honeymoon destination dreams dating back to junior high. She had carefully clipped travel brochures and wedding magazine and newspaper clippings of exotic, fantastic vacation destinations for newly-weds. The scrapbook was an overflowing, spine-splitting hodge-podge of dreams. Now she had a chance to make her dreams become reality.

Brad had asked her to become his bride the next June. Suddenly, the scrapbook of clippings was full of possible realities. But where to start? Where does one go for the perfect honeymoon? Travel agencies, bride's guides and the Internet are crammed full of fancy packages with inviting marketing for fabulous honeymoon trips. You can find dozens and dozens of travel guides and books for your honeymoon. But don't start there.

Your honeymoon is not about the place. It's about the two of you and about your love. It's about your new life together as a family and getting started on the right foot. Take the 15-day European coach tour for your fifth anniversary. Mission trip to Uganda? Another time. A fancy 7- to 10-day cruise through the Caribbean? Well, maybe. But immediately following your wedding, may we suggest that you start with a simple getaway where the two of you can mostly just enjoy being together *privately*, taking it easy and doing something that the two of you love to do together?

We emphasize the word "privately" because there is nothing like booking the perfect little bed and breakfast honeymoon suite for the week, only to discover that the walls (and floor) are as thin and creaky as any other old house from the early nineteenth century, and all your meals will be shared with all the other inhabitants of the house sitting across the table from the two of you . . . after a few nights of honeymoon bedroom activities that kept the rest of them awake and left little to the imagination. That little bed and breakfast might look great in the brochures, but we promise that you will want something a bit more private, a bit more anonymous.

Simple is good. Privacy makes it great. Some of the best honeymoons we've heard about were some of the most extraordinarily simple.

One couple went to great lengths to keep their wedding night and honeymoon destination a secret. They packed their bags, closed up their house, got married and left from the reception in the limo, which took them right back to their new home, where they spent the next five days in uninterrupted marital bliss! They reserved a more elaborate travel time to be enjoyed two months later. Without knowing it, they were following a centuries-old tradition.

Caroline and Jeremy were exhausted after the busy, hectic weeks of preparation and entertaining of friends and family before their large, formal wedding. Wisely, they chose to follow the advice of good friends and decided to have a simple, quiet, inexpensive and restful honeymoon in a family member's condominium in the nearby mountains—just a couple of hours from home.

Caroline says, "We spent our first honeymoon week resting and focusing inward. We only left the condo two times the whole week!" Jeremy adds, "On day two, Caroline was still so exhausted that she slept for about 15 hours—and would have slept longer except that I woke her up to join me for the rest of the day!"

Four months later, the refreshed and relaxed couple traveled to New Zealand and Fiji. Caroline says, "We were *so* glad we waited. It gave us time to save money, plan our trip and figure out how to live together. Overseas traveling was a splendid adventure we could share, but travel like that is also *demanding*. We are *so* glad we didn't attempt that our first week together—when rest, inward focus and figuring out sex pretty much took all our energy."

I have had friends and patients choose a simple seaside cottage or remote mountain cabin. The less activity planned and the simpler the plans, the better the honeymoon.

When I practiced in the Kissimmee, Florida, area, I would have patients and friends who booked rooms that were designed for honeymooners in our tourist area for several days. They blended into the vacationers like any other visitor to our hometown and had a marvelous honeymoon—no jet lag, no luggage lost on flights changing through multiple cities, no schedule to keep for tourist events, no problems speaking the language or exchanging currency, no traveler's diarrhea, no seasickness, no big honeymoon credit-card debt.

For Richard and Elizabeth, it was five days at a secluded mountain cabin only an hour from where they were married. For Patrick and Sally, it was a couple of nights in the honeymoon suite of a hotel near the wedding site, before flying off to Disney World. Jim and Nancy chose to be in their apartment for a few days before traveling. My son, Scott, and his new wife, Jennifer, chose the honeymoon suite of a nearby hotel, with a sumptuous Ruth's Chris Steakhouse dinner delivered to and served in their private suite, before heading out of town later in the week.

In each of these cases, the honeymooners simply had privacy, plenty of uninterrupted time together, a great bed, and home-grown hospitality.

Those who were in touristy areas had lots of entertainment options *if* they decided they wanted to do something other than gaze into each other's eyes, rest and spend time together in the hotel room!

As an added bonus, none of these couples started out their marriage with exorbitant credit-card debt from an expensive honeymoon. Yes, it's tempting to go extravagant, but unless it's gifted to you, we recommend staying within your means—what you have saved and can afford. It will be one less stress on your early married life—and, as Karen and Tom learned, an expensive trip doesn't ensure a happy honeymoon (and that goes double for the wedding!)

You'll find at the end of this chapter some helpful planning tools and recommendations for a simple honeymoon. Then, just in case you have your heart set on something a bit more exotic, we've also included plenty of tips and helpful tools for preparing for long-distance or international travel. We've opted to stick with convention and structure honeymoon planning around a seven-day trip, but feel free to shorten or extend your plans to suit your calendar and budget.

You'll note that there are no plans at all in this book for bringing others along with you on your honeymoon—children from prior relationships, friends or family. That's an intentional omission. The honeymoon is a time for you and your spouse to establish the base and underpinning for your marriage relationship—alone, without distraction from others. Period.

Set the foundation of your marriage well with *only* the two of you, and children and family will fall into line at a later time. Get off to a rocky start and you'll risk the possibility of carrying the wounds or scars long into your relationship—and run the risk of negatively affecting or even wrecking the rest of your marriage.

Horror Stories

Wreck the rest of your marriage? Does that sound a bit dramatic? Unfortunately, we have each seen more than our fair share of couples whose beginning of the end for their marriage was, ironically, during the very first week—during the honeymoon.

You want horror stories? We've heard them all, and our hearts are set on helping you, as a couple, get your marriage off to a happier start.

Ken and Sue's dating had been tumultuous. Friends were actually surprised when they began to talk about marriage—but even more surprised at the very short engagement. To plan a large, fancy wedding with several hundred guests in less than four months is almost impossible, but somehow, they pulled it off. The evening wedding was followed by a several-hour drive to their honeymoon suite. If only Tom had had time to get his car serviced before the trip. When the car broke down, they were not within range of a cell phone tower. They finally arrived at their honeymoon hotel at about 3:15 A.M. and needed to be up at 5:00 A.M. to have time to get to the airport for their 9:00 A.M. flight.

The 16-hour flight to Australia was crowded, and their seats, which would not lean back, miserably uncomfortable. Worst of all, their jet lag and exhaustion, combined with no premarital counseling or honeymoon planning, mixed with two volatile personality disorders that had been cleverly disguised during their dating and engagement, led to a week of nonstop bickering, arguing, fighting and feuding.

The complexity of their relationship combined with a complex set of wedding and honeymoon plans drilled holes in the hull of their marriage ship long before it left dock. To no one's surprise, the marriage quickly sank.

For John and Sandy, the marriage broke apart seven years after their disastrous honeymoon. The story is long and convoluted, but the bottom line is the same—failure to prepare for a spiritual honeymoon created a flawed foundation whose cracks became more and more apparent as the years went by.

Please understand that we share these horror stories not because they are rare but because in our practices they have been far too common. We *know* that you would do anything to avoid a similar shipwreck, right? What you really want is a honeymoon that will continue on beyond the first week.

Your honeymoon is designed to be just about the two of you—to be the solid foundation for a lifelong, satisfying and significant marriage. Your honeymoon is not about pleasing your family and friends; rather, it's about setting the foundation in the first week of your marriage for a long, happy and love-filled marriage.

General Planning Tips

Unlike other vacations, when planning the honeymoon of a lifetime, you want to maximize your time focusing on each other; therefore, here are some general considerations:

1. The hotel accommodation is of primary importance. A honeymoon without privacy or a quiet, secluded and comfortable bedroom is not going to be much fun for either of you.

2. Decrease travel complications—get to where you are going quickly, with all of your luggage, and stay there for the whole honeymoon.

3. Choose a location where there are activities that you *both* enjoy and a location that allows you privacy and plenty of time for each other.

Sue and Dale went to a ski resort for their honeymoon. They had great accommodations and the resort had plenty of good restaurants and shopping. They enjoyed a bit of fun on the slopes together, and lots of fun in the hot tub after skiing. Barb and I went to a warmer honeymoon location—the then newly opened Disney World. Our on-site hotel was secluded and quiet, had beaches, pools, romantic restaurants, walking paths and quaint shops; yet we could easily and quickly get into the various parks whenever we were ready to do so without the hassle of driving, traffic and parking. And both the Larimores and the Crocketts did this as students on a student's budget!

Since those dreamy days so many years ago, Sue and I have gathered dozens of travel tips from our patients, friends and those we have counseled about their honeymoon experiences. We hope this information will give you tons of great ideas and save you many headaches, heart-aches and disappointments.

Simple Honeymoon Plan for Seven Days

No matter where you finally end up on your honeymoon, you'll find that people *love* honeymooners and will want to do special things for you. Don't be embarrassed to let them know. Before you arrive at your destination—when you are traveling there and when you check in—let the staff know that you are on your honeymoon. This almost always leads to memorable and unexpected surprises.

We recommend that you consider using a reputable travel agent. Yes, we know that you can do it all yourself on the Internet. Neverthe-less, we still think it's critical for honeymoon travel to have profes-sional guidance. If there are *any* complications, one call to your travel agent can save hours or days of disappointment. Besides, most travel agents don't charge a fee, so take advantage of their services and spare yourself a lot of research time and work when you don't have lots of time available. Choose someone you trust with whom you or family members have worked and have been pleased. Another option is to get recommendations for a travel agent from your pastor or friends.

We suggest that if you don't know the agent, arrange to meet the agent in person. Be sure to give the agent a firm budget range and some desir-able dream destinations that both you and your fiancé are interested in.

Oh, by the way, whenever exploring travel options, be sure to ask about honeymoon package deals. These deals almost always include complimentary upgraded accommodations, special check-in arrange-ments, checkout privileges and much more.

Here are some of our favorite honeymoon travel tips. *Within a 100-mile radius* of the city in which you will be married:

- Drive your own car.
- Book an upgrade hotel room or suite with a large, comfortable bed in an area known for privacy or tourism, depending on your preferences. Many hotels have honeymoon suites.

- In tourist areas, you will be able to find good restaurants, shopping and other entertainment activities.
- In private cabins, you need to either bring supplies or rent a cabin that is well supplied.

In appendix B, we've gathered even more resources to help you plan your honeymoon. There's a section for foreign travel and more extravagant honeymoon packages. There are gobs of packing tips to help you plan way in advance, and a master packing list for the honeymoon.

But, most of all, don't forget to pack your sense of humor and a big sense of adventure. The fact is that with most travel these days, there will be plenty of unexpected surprises. Expect these bumps in the road and face each one, arm in arm, together.

No matter what happens, love will get you through it and you'll come home with tons of memories that you (and your future kids) will be able to look back on and laugh about.

For Thought and Prayer

1. Picture your first night together as husband and wife. What do you dream of? Where do you want to be? What will it take to get there?

2. Since you've now been introduced to the idea of a honeymoon as a different trip from other vacations, how have your plans changed? What will you plan differently from just a regular vacation or a typical honeymoon?

3. Is the idea of resting a few days before leaving town an option? Have you planned time just to rest, sleep and spend private time together? If not, what do you need to do?

4. Is there any merit to waiting a few weeks or months for a fancy honeymoon? What locations and activities would you both enjoy?

5. How and when do you plan to implement each of these decisions?

Resources

Fares and Reservations
CheapTickets	www.cheaptickets.com
Expedia	www.expedia.com
Hotwire	www.hotwire.com
Orbitz	www.orbitz.com
Priceline	www.priceline.com
Side Step	www.sidestep.com
Travelocity	www.travelocity.com

Useful Travel Information
Exchange Rates	www.x-rates.com
Intellicast (weather)	www.intellicast.com
CDC Travelers' Health	www.cdc.gov/travel
Travel Health Online	www.tripprep.com

Travel Guides
Fodor's Travel Online	www.fodors.com
Frommer's	www.frommers.com
Lonely Planet	www.lonelyplanet.com
National Park Service	www.nps.gov
Rough Guides	www.roughguides.com
Travel Advisor	www.traveladvisor.com
Travel Notes	www.travelnotes.org

Part Two

Chapter Eight

FOR THE BRIDE'S EYES ONLY

Older women likewise are to be reverent in their behavior . . .
teaching what is good, so that they may encourage the
young women to love their husbands.

TITUS 2:3-4, *NASB*

Brenda was one short week away from her honeymoon when I invited her to lunch at my (Sue's) house.[1] We sat down to a table set with my great-grandmother's linens, my husband's grandmother's silver, and my grandmother's gold-rimmed tea glasses. This was a wonderful meeting—a rite of passage, a time of handing down of ageless advice from one generation to the next, a story told by an older woman to a younger woman, the thread carrying on down through the ages, much like my family's heirlooms, mother to daughter to successive daughter again.

Only Brenda wasn't my daughter—she was one of my patients and a close family friend from church. She had chosen to remain sexually pure until her wedding night—and it was less than a week away. What a privilege it was to be asked by her mother to share this special time with Brenda as she prepared for her wedding and her honeymoon.

There were some advantages, of course, to my not being Brenda's mother. I imagine this role may have been commonly filled in ages past by a wise aunt or grandmother. There are some things that are just not as easily discussed with your own mother. But with me, Brenda had a chance to ask all the questions she was wondering about—some of them quite practical, some of them profound and some of them not quite so serious. As we talked, she often giggled nervously. I answered her as truthfully and frankly as I knew how. We laughed and talked and put her nerves at ease about her new role as Adam's wife. It was a beautiful afternoon.

How I wish I could spend this special time with each and every one of my patients approaching their honeymoon. It's a ritual largely lost in our society of pop-culture media, sex, school health classes, technology and fragmented families. This rite of passage is sorely needed by all women regardless of when they decide to become sexually active. The responsibility for these discussions, however, falls more and more on the medical profession, yet a busy office is hardly the setting for this type of intimate discussion. So the time-honored ritual falls through the cracks of our society, lost to most in this generation—but fortunately, *not* to you. You see, I've personally written this chapter to *you*—woman to woman. This chapter is not meant to be read until a week or two before your wedding—similar to the timing of my luncheon with Brenda. I have included questions gathered not only from years of discussions with my patients but also from the wisdom of other women who have taught me, women older and wiser than me, women who've been there, done that—some well and some not so well. This is the advice they and I wish to pass on to you.

In preparing to write this chapter for you, I surveyed hundreds of married women and asked them what they would have wanted to know going into marriage—and what they would like me to pass on to you. Many of their replies had something to do with sex, sexual intimacy or the honeymoon in particular. We've discussed many of those concerns in the previous chapters. A surprising number of women had horrible experiences on their honeymoon with honeymoon cystitis and wanted to make sure that we addressed that issue in particular in this book. Many, many others testified to how placing God at the center of the honeymoon helped launch the richest and happiest marriages. So I thought you might want to have some of the wisdom from these women, written from our hearts to yours.

The Honeymoon

First of all, relax! Make having fun and enjoying getting to know each other as husband and wife your primary priority. The rest will fall in line much easier if you take the pressure off performance!

If you consummate your marriage on your wedding night—great! If you don't, that's okay too. Expect your wedding night to be incredible because you are finally married and together, but let go of the expectation that it will be the most fabulous sexual experience ever. You have a whole lifetime to grow and learn about each other. The marriage consummation is a beginning, not an endpoint.

In fact, in my medical practice, I've had many, many couples that did not have intercourse on their wedding night, for one reason or another. Some of them were just plain exhausted or had already had sex together, so it wasn't a priority.

Many of these couples were not sexually experienced and were not comfortable jumping in so fast. They took their time over the honeymoon week, gradually gaining familiarity with each other's bodies and sexual preferences, consummating a day or two into the marriage.

A very few have returned to my office after the honeymoon unable to consummate the marriage due to a stubbornly intact hymen or other sexual dysfunction. Even these couples, though, in the context of a loving and highly spiritual marriage, found creative ways to have a healthy sex life, despite not being able to have vaginal intercourse—although I certainly helped them fix the problem quickly! And for many, having the premarital examination we discussed in chapter 6 would have prevented most of these problems.

What did these couples have in common? They all realized that sex is a wonderful part of a healthy marriage and sex on your honeymoon is a very fun thing, but it's only the beginning. It gets even better with time.

In fact, it would be helpful to extend this concept to the honeymoon in general. Whether you have a fabulous honeymoon trip or one filled with challenges, it's simply *not* the whole marriage. It's just the beginning, and it gets better with time when you work together as a loving couple in the context of the divine design for your honeymoon and marriage.

Honeymoon Kit!

One of my favorite things about being a gynecologist is getting to take care of women preparing for marriage. They, like you, are full of anticipation, hope, joy and excitement about the prospects of the honeymoon and the marriage. For those who have remained virginal, there is often special nervousness about sexual intimacy and the honeymoon itself.

In talking with these women, I have realized that having a plan and being prepared is an important part of settling these jitters and giving my patients confidence about their sexuality and their wedding night. Through the years, both Walt and I, independent of each other, began compiling a suggested list of helpful items for our patients to pack and take on their honeymoon—what we call the Honeymoon Kit.

Most of the items suggested in this chapter will not be needed—but if you *do* need them, you'll be glad you packed them. There is comfort in knowing that you can take care of many of the minor problems that could arise on your trip. Most of my female patients return giggling from their honeymoon, never having needed to use most items they took along with them. Nevertheless, a good many of the kit contents will find their way into your marriage routine, as you might find them useful on a regular basis.

For our patients, Walt and I break down the kit contents into two sections: Setting the Mood and Female Health Items. We include in the packing list an explanation and instructions for using the various items. The items on the list are only suggestions. Feel free to personalize the list for yourself.

We recommend that you review the list with your doctor. For your convenience, we have provided you with a shopping/packing list for your Honeymoon Kit, complete with brief instructions that you can copy and pack with your supplies. This list is located in appendix A.

I have created Honeymoon Kits for friends in a variety of assorted containers—fancy boxes, treasure chests, and baskets all make a nice presentation. But practically speaking, a nice-sized waterproof cosmetic bag probably works just as well—the kind that has two sides with matching zip compartments, with clear plastic windows, or the ones that open up like a book and make it easy to see and retrieve the items packed. I've found these bags reasonably priced in the cosmetic section of local pharmacies and grocery stores.

You can also find gift kits with some of the mood items we recommend preassembled. Stores such as *Bath and Body Works* sell sets such as these with bubble bath, bath lotions and soaps in wonderfully scented collections, including a cosmetic bag as packaging. Take the full-sized items out of these bags, keeping them for your use after returning from the honeymoon, and replace them with smaller travel-sized counterparts for the Honeymoon Kit, which will also leave more room to fit in other items.

Sexual Intimacy Preparations

"Preparing for sex? It takes preparation? You mean I can't just jump into bed and do it?" Well, of course you *can*! And your desire for your husband after all this time of anticipation may be so great that you don't even want to think about anything else!

However, you may want to give some thought to planning your time together. Keep it interesting and keep him guessing what you'll come up with next. A new outfit? A different ambiance? A back rub? Never let your sex life fall into a rut.

In order to fulfill this advice, there is one very important thing you must do. You must choose to be an active participant! Don't just lay there and expect him to do all the work! Not only is that *not* much fun for you, but it's not nearly as much fun for him either—at least not as much fun as having a partner who acts as though she's interested in what's going on! He needs to know that you find him attractive, and one of the best things you can do to boost his confidence as a man is to show him how appreciative you are of him sexually. It's part of the "respecting him" part of you that we've already discussed.

Sexual fulfillment is not just about satisfying him—it's about you too! Being an active participant in sex ensures that he learns what fulfills you sexually, and it increases your chances of orgasm. What man doesn't want to be able to sexually satisfy his wife?

Therefore, it's important to make the effort to set the mood for sexual intimacy with your new husband. You've probably already begun to prepare by shopping for personal and lingerie items, as well as ensuring privacy and a romantic setting for your wedding night!

Let's just take a minute and pack a few items to make the mood extra special. Think about what you and your spouse may find relaxing or fun. We've started the list with some obvious items and encourage you, as a couple, to add your own. And, of course, strawberries and chocolate are a classic!

Write a Love Letter

You need to prepare your most important sexual organ for the experience—you need to prepare your brain. We talked about this in chapter 4.

The *Merriam-Webster Dictionary* gives three definitions for the word "intercourse." The first is "connection or dealings between persons or groups." The second, like unto it, is "exchange especially of thoughts or feelings: communion." It's only the third definition that resonates with what was likely on your mind: "physical sexual contact between individuals that involves the genitalia of at least one person."[2]

So take some time before your wedding and write a love letter to your future husband to read together on your wedding night. What do you love most about him? What do you find most physically attractive about him? What characteristics do you most admire? What attributes and qualities about him do you most respect? How do you feel about being married to him? Are there any significant Scriptures you would like to include?

It might take several drafts to get your letter just right, but you will finally be able to write the final draft. I recommend that you *write* this letter by hand—don't type or print it. Written letters are *so* much more romantic, don't you think? Fold and seal your love letter and then pack it in your Honeymoon Kit to read to him later.

Pack Other Mood Items

Candle and Matches—I particularly like candles for setting the mood— sweet fragrance, nice ambiance. A little soft light, revealing enough to allow some visualization—so important to the sexual experience, *especially* for men—subtle enough, ladies, to be comfortably concealing, even for the most modest of us. A small votive-sized candle or tea light in a votive glass is easily packed and won't present a fire hazard. Plan on picking up a small lighter or pack of matches so that when you reach your destination, you'll be able to use your candle! (Lighters and matches cannot be carried through security checks at airports.)

Bubble Bath, Soaps and/or Bath Oil—A nice, relaxing bath in sweetly scented bubbles works equally well for a bit of private relaxation in preparation for your intimate time together—or for both of you to enjoy together.

One word of caution: If you have any pain with urination, or vaginal irritation, scented or dyed products may intensify the problem. In this case, lose the bubble bath and scented soaps; stick to mild, unscented, non-deodorant and non-antibacterial soaps when washing, and replace the bubbles with a half cup of baking soda dissolved in warm bath water.

Body Lotions or Massage Oil—Whether you are experienced sexually or not, a full body massage for each other is a great way to say "hello" in the bedroom. Not only is it a gentle, nonthreatening way for newlyweds to get to know each other's bodies, but it's also a very relaxing, enjoyable activity.

In his chapter to your fiancé, Walt will let your husband-to-be know that this may be more important for you than for him. He'll tell the guys that it's well worth taking their time here, as massage can be an incredibly potent foreplay activity, heightening the sexual experience for you both.

K-Y Warming Liquid lubricant, which can be found in most grocery stores or pharmacies in the aisle near the feminine products (condoms, yeast medications, and pregnancy test kits) is a product that combines a self-warming water-based massage oil and personal lubricant. Good combination, if you ask me.

Personal Lubricant—Women have the natural ability to create ample self-lubricant when sexually aroused. However, vaginal dryness doesn't necessarily indicate lack of sexual desire or inadequate foreplay. More commonly it could indicate a nervous, dehydrated or tired bride on a honeymoon. Lubrication can certainly help.

Part of the pleasure in intercourse is that it *is* a friction-causing activity. However, this is definitely one of those cases where too much of a good thing puts a damper on even the most satisfying sex. Too much friction without lubrication, especially early in the honeymoon, and your sexual encounters will dwindle or become more uncomfortable toward the latter part of your honeymoon.

For women, especially virginal women, vaginal soreness and chafing or even mild bleeding is common during or after sex on the honeymoon. Even for previously experienced couples, the high frequency of intercourse potentially encountered during a week of honeymoon recreation can lead to discomfort—for men too! So be sure and pack a lubricant.

Which one to choose? In addition to being slick, sexual lubricants should be water-based, such as K-Y Jelly or Astroglide. Avoid petroleum-based products made from petroleum jelly, mineral oil or petrolatum—such as Vaseline products and baby oils. Petroleum-based lubricants can destroy or melt latex—practically on contact. Therefore, they should never be used with condoms, diaphragms or cervical caps. Also, petroleum-based lubricants can stain fabric and can be difficult to wash out. Petroleum-based products can also irritate the vagina and trap bacteria—both of which can increase your risk of vaginitis or vaginal infection. You should never use these products as vaginal lubricants.

Another group of products to avoid are oil-based products that are usually made from natural products, such as vegetable oils, nut oils, Crisco or butter. Like petroleum-based products, oil-based lubricants can stain fabrics and can be difficult to wash off, but are safer for vaginal use. And oil-based lubricants also destroy latex, so they should not be used with condoms, diaphragms or cervical caps.

Which products do I recommend? Astroglide—a water-based, silicon-like product first developed (so I am told) by a rocket scientist. This chemist discovered the super slippery polymeric compound while working to create oils for the space shuttle's moving parts. Astroglide can be found over the counter, near the condoms. Our patients swear by this stuff. And to compete with the aforementioned K-Y Warming Liquid, the manufacturer of Astroglide is now marketing Astroglide Warming Liquid.

In addition to K-Y Warming Liquid lubricant, K-Y makes a full line of lubricating gels. One of them, K-Y with nonoxyl-9, contains spermicide in addition to lubrication. Using this product in conjunction with a condom or diaphragm may improve the birth control effect and also provide a second line of defense against unintended pregnancy in case of breakage or slippage.

A word of caution: Nonoxyl-9 carries with it a risk of allergic reaction or hypersensitivity. Please test it on your hand prior to slathering it on for sexual fun. An allergic reaction during intercourse, especially on the honeymoon, is not a pretty thing.

Female Health Items

Birth Control—Be sure to read our discussion of the potential ethical concerns about hormonal birth control in chapter 6. Once you make your decision about your choice of birth control, don't forget to pack it with you for your wedding night and honeymoon. If you are taking a daily medication, don't forget to take it consistently, especially if going through significant time changes on your trip.

Tampons or Pads—You may have timed your honeymoon to avoid your monthly menses, taking advantage of our recommendations in chapter 6 concerning menstrual shifting or manipulation, or you may have made the decision to stop your periods medically. Just in case, though, stash a few tampons or pads in your Honeymoon Kit.

Honeymoon Vaginitis Relief—I've already mentioned the risk of vaginal irritation from intercourse during the honeymoon. In my survey, and in my medical practice, vaginitis is the number-one medical condition for honeymoon couples. Honeymoon vaginitis or vaginal irritation may present with burning, chafing or mild swelling of the labia. In order to help ease that discomfort, should it occur, you might want to pack a few items.

The first line of treatment is a cool compress, such as a washcloth, found in most hotel facilities. You shouldn't have to pack that. The next step for cooling things down is an ice pack. Therefore, I recommend packing a zip-lock baggie. Most hotels have an ice machine readily accessible. To make a quick and effective ice pack, fill the zip-lock baggie with ice, wrap it in a cloth (don't forget to do that and risk getting frostbite), and have a seat. Ahhh! Relief!

Be sure to take a little bit of pain reliever along with it. As we've mentioned, we're partial to ibuprofen (Motrin or Advil) over acetaminophen (Tylenol) for its better anti-inflammatory properties.

Baking soda is another vaginal relief trick. It's inexpensive and comes in small boxes in the grocery store. Pour a half-cup or so in a tub of warm water and take a nice relaxing bath. Leave out the bubble bath or soaps. Just soak in the baking soda. Vaginal irritation due to slightly acidic bacterial overgrowth, like *lactobacillus*, responds especially well to this treatment.

Irritation from yeast infection, also an acidic vaginal pH condition, may be somewhat neutralized by the basic properties of a baking soda bath although not usually cured by such.

Honeymoon Cystitis Relief—Honeymoon cystitis is a bladder infection (or urinary tract infection) that happens as a result of sexual activity and is caused by bacteria traveling up the urethra and into the bladder. In my survey, second only to honeymoon vaginitis, urinary tract infections are common, especially in couples that have not been sexually active previously.

To prevent cystitis, empty your bladder within 15 to 20 minutes following intercourse to flush out the bacteria from the urethra. Just in case this doesn't work and you think you may have cystitis, it may be identified by the following symptoms:

- painful and/or frequent urination—but keep in mind that minor abrasions from sexual activity may also be responsible for external urinary discomfort,
- foul-smelling urine, and/or
- pain or cramping above the pubic bone.

I recommend that you pack some Uristat, an over-the-counter urinary pain reliever. This medication concentrates itself in the bladder, buying you a bit of relief until either the antibiotic takes effect or you can find a medical facility. By packing a prefilled antibiotic prescription, such as generic forms of Macrodantin or Bactrim (both of which specifically treat urinary tract infections), you should be able to treat an early infection and avoid the potential nightmare of honeymoon cystitis.

Also, pure cranberry juice, long noted as a housewife's cure for urinary tract infections, may be helpful if taken early in the course of an infection. Cranberries contain hippuric acid, a natural compound that prevents the bacteria responsible for cystitis from being able to hold on to the bladder wall. Capsules containing dried cranberry powder are easier to pack.

Fever or back (kidney) pain may signal a more serious urinary tract infection. Onset of these symptoms requires medical attention and you should *not* attempt to self-treat these symptoms.

Vaginal Yeast Infection Relief—Yeast thrives in moist environments. Travel, perspiration, stress and changes in diet all make the honeymoon a particularly common time to contract yeast—so the honeymoon is a fertile ground for this problem.

A vaginal yeast infection is usually easily treated with a vaginal yeast medication. For convenience, we recommend buying an over-the-counter version, such as Monistat, in the single-dose version. Or you can have your physician write a prescription for Diflucan, a one-dose oral medication that's very convenient but somewhat expensive. As I mentioned above, a baking-soda bath may help ease the irritation from a yeast infection.

Answers to Questions You Can't Just Ask Anywhere

This section is devoted to answering questions that women have asked me over the years in the privacy of my medical office. Just in case you were wondering . . .

Q: Is having sex going to hurt?
A: It might, especially after repeated intercourse during the honeymoon. It's common even for nonvirginal women to experience minor

abrasions, labial swelling or even bleeding from the friction. Discomfort with the first sexual experience differs from woman to woman on an individual basis, and it is influenced by a multitude of factors, including anatomy, preparation, lubrication and state of mind.

In the most basic terms, pain with the first sexual encounter for a woman is most commonly associated with the physical action of the penis entering the opening of the vagina, an area that can be quite sensitive and may be narrowed by the hymen.

The integrity of the hymen, a thin ring (usually) of connective tissue, circling the opening to the vagina, historically has been thought to be proof of virginity. However, in today's society, with young women physically active in sports and using tampons during menstruation, the hymen is commonly not intact even in most virginal females. As the hymen is stretched or torn during sexual contact, some discomfort, or even spotting, may occur.

There are some things that a virginal woman can do to help prepare for intercourse and that even sexually experienced women can do to decrease the chance of having pain.

1. Begin Using Tampons

Using tampons may help you become comfortable with something being inserted into the vagina and may help to desensitize this otherwise sensitive area. Start with the very thin ones—Slims—and then gradually work your way up to larger ones, gently dilating the vaginal opening as you progress. Be sure to insert the tampon completely into the vagina, as one that protrudes through the hymen to the outside can become *quite* uncomfortable. You should notice that the tampon, when properly inserted, can barely be perceived.

2. See Your Personal Physician

You need to go to your doctor's office anyway (see the calendar timeline), so why not schedule today? Most women have no problem having a speculum examination done—an examination of the vagina and cervix done by the physician using an instrument to help visualize the cervix and do a Pap smear.

Chances are, if you've had a speculum examination, the hymen is not going to be a problem with intercourse. Very rarely, women may have a hymen that is larger, covering the vaginal opening. If so, a visit to your personal physician will allow the doctor the ability not only to identify this problem but also to fix it for you in plenty of time for the honeymoon.

In 15 years of medical practice, I have only had two patients that I can remember who came to see me after six months or so of marriage because they were still physically unable to consummate their marriage due to a stubborn hymen. Both of them were easily treated with a minor surgical procedure called a hymenotomy—a procedure done under light anesthesia in which the hymen is surgically divided so that intercourse can occur.

3. Consider Stretching the Vaginal Opening/Hymen

This can be done quite easily, and without pain, by a woman preparing for marriage. Using lubricant, insert your thumb just into the vaginal opening and push down gently, towards your rectum. By starting this exercise in the weeks leading up to the honeymoon, not only does the vaginal opening become more accustomed to contact, but also the opening can be gently enlarged to decrease discomfort from intercourse.

4. Learn to Control Your Pelvic Muscles

These muscles, commonly called PC muscles (for pubococcygeous muscles), encircle the openings of the urethra (where your urine comes out), the vagina and the anus. These muscles are somewhat linked together in a "sling" that extends from the pubic bone to the sacrum (the tail bone). Because they are skeletal muscles, like the muscles in your arms or legs, they are capable of being controlled and trained.

Learn to control these muscles first by squeezing your anal muscles. If you've never tried to do this before, it can seem quite difficult! One way to tell if you are doing it correctly is to wrap your finger in a clean piece of toilet paper after finishing using the restroom and place your finger on the outside of your anus as you contract the muscles. If you're doing the exercise properly, you'll feel the muscle contracting.

Once you are able to do this exercise, try practicing without using the bathroom tissue. Try 10 squeezes, each held for two to three seconds.

When you are practicing, nobody should be able to tell you are doing them—there should be no abdominal muscle movement, butt clenching or breath holding if you are doing them correctly! You've now learned to do what we doctors call Kegel exercises!

Now, it may seem counterintuitive to teach about Kegel exercises for preparing for intercourse, as they are commonly used to strengthen vaginal muscles, which would make the vaginal opening tighter. But once you learn control of these muscles, you can also concentrate on *relaxing* them in order to decrease the amount of pressure during intercourse.

Going one step beyond that, these muscles are also commonly called the love muscles, and women are capable of learning to contract them in such a manner as to enhance the sexual pleasure for themselves and their partner.

5. Use Lots of Lubricant

In fact, I recommend that if you will be having your first sexual intercourse on the honeymoon, that you absolutely use a lubricant.

Plan to put it on him. It will increase his excitement and provide some protection from irritation for you both. You'll appreciate this advice later in the week—when neither of you have irritation in your genital area.

Often, women will find that the discomfort is mainly with entrance of the penis into the vagina and lessens once it is actually in. You can help ease this by actively guiding him into place and taking control of his initial entry—and the lubricant will help here. For many women, this is easiest if you are on top of him. Dr. Walt will explain this to the men in his chapter, so don't be surprised if your husband suggests this position initially!

6. Take a Pain Reliever

Take a pain reliever such as ibuprofen, unless you have a medical reason that you should not take this class of medications, which also has anti-inflammatory properties to decrease swelling.

There are plenty of things you can do as a virginal female to prepare physically for your first sexual experience. The most important thing, though, is to approach it with joy and confidence and not with fear. Learning to think positively about sex with your husband is the most important part!

Let your desire be for your husband. Think about (and tell him) what you find physically attractive about him. Choose an attitude toward sex of anticipation and of mutually shared joy. God created you to love each other physically, emotionally and spiritually. Have fun with the physical!

Q: How often is it "normal" to have or want sex?
A: In general, this varies greatly. People with very different sex drives often end up joined together in marriage, with the expectation that their partner will have the same libido. This is not usually the case! Sex drives seem to come in three common categories, and they are all normal!

1. Daily or more than once a day
2. Weekly or several times a week
3. Monthly or less

You need to know that it is common for couples *not* to have the same sexual needs! Just because your husband wants sex more (or less) frequently does not necessarily mean that there is something wrong with either one of you—it's likely just a difference in your natural sex drive. Nevertheless, unrecognized and not dealt with, this difference can cause big problems in a marriage, with lots of misunderstandings. Being sensitive to each other's natural needs will help alleviate some of these issues.

Along these lines, a very wise woman, who was a once-a-monther married to a once-a-weeker gave me the following advice: "What if he's in the mood and I'm not? Then I make the choice to 'play' anyway. I make the choice even if I don't necessarily feel like it. It makes him happy and . . . sometimes . . . once we get started, I find out that I will all of a sudden be in the mood! Now that's a win-win proposition!"

Remember, there are lots of ways to make him happy that don't necessarily mean sexual intercourse. Sex play can be fun for him and very satisfying.

Q: What about vaginal secretions?
A: Yep, they happen. Barring infections, which can have quite foul discharges and bad odors, you are supposed to have them. Vaginal secretions are a combination of mucous, natural lubricants and natural immune factors. They are secreted from the cervix, vaginal walls and small glands around the opening of the vagina and are an important factor in sexual activity. Vaginal secretions naturally increase with sexual stimulation, mainly due to increased blood flow to the vagina and labia, which may swell noticeably with stimulation. Don't try to douche them away!

Q: Well, okay, but what about the odor?
A: Yep, that happens also. However, you may be surprised to learn that the vast majority of men actually love that musky smell, so don't try to scrub it away with douches and perfumes. You are *not* unclean. Your scent is part of what attracts your husband to you, even on a subconscious level.

Q: What about sex during menses?
A: Important question. This is considered taboo by some religions. Christian writers debate the topic; while some say it is forbidden by the Bible, others say it is acceptable.[3] Yet, I have been surprised how many couples think nothing of it. Aside from being messy, there are two potential medical reasons to avoid this practice. The first is a slightly increased risk of endometritis (infection of the lining of the uterus). The second concerns failure of natural family planning. In women with short menstrual cycles, ovulation may actually occur toward the end of menstruation, resulting in an unintended pregnancy. Nevertheless, most couples have no problem with sex during menses, as long as both are comfortable with it emotionally and spiritually.

Q: What about different sexual positions and/or activities?

A: **For this question, it's helpful to set some ground rules going into marriage,** since women and men often have different expectations about sexual activities.

Many of the women I have talked to have a mutual agreement policy regarding sexual experimentation in the bedroom. Trying new things together is part of a marriage that grows and evolves. Although it's not necessary, it often is part of the journey. Different sexual positions can be necessary to avoid discomfort or to achieve climax.

In addition, what you think is acceptable now may not be in the future. Conversely, what you find objectionable now may seem like fun someday. Hebrews 13:4 states that the marriage bed is undefiled. Sure, God sees all, but He made you to enjoy your spouse sexually. If you and your husband are both comfortable and enjoying yourselves, God is pleased too. Any activities in your sexual life are okay as long as they are within God's divine design (only between the two of you) and mutually agreed on. No physical activity or sexual experimentation that is uncomfortable to you is acceptable. Period.

On another topic, try to remember that his sexual responses are much faster than yours. Help him help you by reminding him there's *no* need to rush. If you sense he's going too fast for you, encourage him to slow down and verbally let him know you appreciate when he does!

However, let me give you a warning—for some men, especially virgins, the pressure of the wedding can be too much and result in two very, very common first-timer sexual dysfunctions. First of all, you and he may discover that his penis is soft and not rock hard. If this is the case the first time or two, absolutely do *not* sweat it. Try to change the mood. Spend some time kissing and fondling him. Perhaps make a game out of how many different body parts you can kiss. Let him massage you. Or you can take a small dab of K-Y Warming Liquid lubricant and give his genitals a massage. He'll love it! As he relaxes and the pressure wears off, he'll respond.

Second, and much more common, many men can actually have premature ejaculation—even before vaginal penetration. If you sense him getting too hot or too worked up too early, slow things down! He'll have *no* trouble "reactivating" after a bit of rest. In fact, you can help him learn to slow down! And, if there's any trouble with this, then you can apply a topical anesthetic containing benzocaine. One over-the-counter gel is called Mandelay. It's marketed in the condom section of the pharmacy as a treatment for men with premature ejaculation. Warning, here—be sure that he uses a condom during intercourse so the anesthetic will not blunt your response!

Q: How often should I have an orgasm?
A: The range of "normal" for women ranges from never having experienced an orgasm to having multiple orgasms each encounter. Some women absolutely have to have an orgasm each time they have sex in order to feel satisfied, and others are very content to have the sexual intimacy without ever climaxing. However, most women fall somewhere in between, along the lines of "most of the time we have sex" or "some of the time, but it's not that important to me to have one *every* time."

In my experience, most women, if asked, will confess to faking it at one time or another in order not to hurt their husband's feelings or because they are just plain tired and ready to go to sleep! Certainly, this is not what I would recommend on a regular basis for a happy, healthy sex life—and especially not on your honeymoon!

Talk with your husband, and encourage him to learn how to bring you to an orgasm. Take the time to communicate to him about your needs and specifically what you find pleasurable. And when he does, make an effort to give up the control of your body to him and relax enough to let him see you have an orgasm.

Most men find the ability to please a woman almost as satisfying as having an orgasm themselves! For more information on techniques for achieving orgasm with your partner, I recommend the three books listed at the end of the chapter.

Q: What about the mess?
A: Yes, sex can be messy. How couples clean up is a very individual thing. One couple I know recommends buying some soft "special" hand

towels that are kept in the bedside table for cleaning up afterward. For some husbands, the subtle signal of a hand towel on the bedside table could set the stage as an invitation for bedtime fun.

Other women recommend using baby wipes or simply showering. Of course, urinating after sex (within 15 to 20 minutes) is a helpful means of preventing cystitis or bladder infections, if you find yourself prone to them. By the way, neither of us recommends routine or frequent douching—which can be damaging over time.

Q: Why do I make a noise like passing gas when we have intercourse?
A: What, you've never heard of a queef? No problem. Neither had Dr. Walt or the physicians who reviewed this book!

Anyway, it is common for air to be forced out of the vagina during intercourse, making a noise similar to passing gas. In fact, this is so common that there is now a word to describe it—"queef." When this happens to you, just laugh together and know that it is something shared by others in the human race. No big deal.

Queefs are more common with certain sexual positions, so varying positions could help fix this leakage.

Speaking of leakage, some women find that a full bladder or rectum during sex actually increases the sexual stimulation, increasing the intensity (or chance of) orgasm. This, of course, is recommended with caution for women with incontinence issues.

Q: What if I don't know what to do or I'm not good at it?
A: Simply put, you don't have to be "good." First of all, being there and being interested in sexual intimacy with your husband is the first step. You just need to be present and thinking about what makes him happy. Ask him what he wants. Let him tell you or show you what turns him on; then you'll be good for him, and he's the only one who counts! Some couples need some additional education in this area. Detailed sexual advice is beyond the scope of this book, but if you need help in this area, I highly recommend the three books listed at the end of this chapter.

The Honeymoon as an Adjustment Period

Besides adjusting to each other physically, the honeymoon is an adjustment period for the two of you to begin to adapt to living with each other.

And beware—for many brides, there is a let-down period following all the hype of the wedding. All of a sudden there is no more rushing about, planning and general business—no more family and friends with you as the center of attention. Now it's just you and him. You and him . . . and sex.

It may seem hard to believe, but it's common to feel bored or let down after the business of planning the wedding, not to mention just the general business of our daily routines! Relax. That's part of what you are supposed to experience on the honeymoon. Rest and unwind from the business of life.

Not only is it okay to miss your family and friends, but it's normal! In the surveys from our older, wiser married women, this issue came up as a bit of a surprise to me. "Most brides, I think, feel a little guilty if they miss their families or friends on the honeymoon," one woman wrote, "but it *is* an artificial situation and they need to know that others feel the same way too."

There's an old folk song called "Billy Boy" in which a man is asked many questions about his bride. At the end of every verse he says, "She's a young thing and cannot leave her mother." But the joke is that she's really an old woman. You may feel a bit scared or uncertain, but you won't be the old woman in this song. It just shows that brides historically have had difficulty leaving their parents' sheltering arms for the strong arms of a loving husband.

You'll be back to your community in a short time. This week is for you to focus on each other. Don't spend all of this precious time wishing for or missing your friends!

The separation from parents and the beginning of your new family may be difficult for your parents too. This is where the in-law nightmares may begin. Now is a perfect time, during the transition period of your honeymoon, to reaffirm your commitment to each other and to agree not to let the in-laws interfere in your relationship.

In Genesis, the very first book of the Bible, we are told, "For this reason a man will *leave* his father and mother and be united to his wife, and they will become one flesh." (Gen. 2:24, emphasis added).

One of my most respected women mentors had this insight to pass on: "Respect that your parents may be having a hard time 'losing you,' but hold firmly to your partner being the *number one* person in your life. This of course doesn't exclude the parents—but changes their role from being totally involved to being a *part* of a new relationship. I think that parents/in-laws create many, many of the problems married couples encounter. This is a delicate balance, blending 'honor your father and mother' with 'a man will leave his father and mother and be united to his wife, and the two will become one flesh.'"

This makes so much sense, and the issue of in-law relations often rears itself on the honeymoon itself. How so? Barring their actually calling you and not respecting your private time together (yes, it happened to one of our virginal survey brides on her wedding night), different families view life differently. You come from different families with different cultures, no matter how similar you think they may seem on the surface. This realization should help you understand why you may approach even some basic issues from different perspectives.

If you've taken the PREPARE or FOCCUS inventories, you are aware of this and how it affects your and your fiancé's families. If you have not taken these inventories, please consider taking one or the other before your wedding. And don't forget, marriage *does* take some getting used to—it's a big change to go from being single to spending your life with someone else! One young bride described it like this: "Going from spending some time together to spending every waking minute together takes some getting used to. You may get on each other's nerves *on* the honeymoon . . . and in the early days. I compare it to what I've heard women complain about when their husbands retire and all of a sudden are home all the time. You love them but aren't used to them being under foot all of the time. You are each bound to irritate the other sooner or later, and it's normal."

Being an Excellent Wife

Since this is the only part in this book where I get to speak just to you women, I thought it important to discuss being an excellent wife in general. It starts with the honeymoon, certainly, but it will take a lifetime to develop. It's a fortunate man who finds a woman who sets her sights on being the best wife she can be starting from the words "I do."

> An excellent wife, who can find? For her worth is far above jewels. The heart of her husband trusts in her, and he will have no lack of gain. She does him good and not evil all the days of her life (Prov. 31:10-12, *NASB*).

It is an amazing responsibility to care for a husband! My favorite Bible passage concerning this issue is Proverbs 31, starting at verse 10. Solomon's words describe a superwoman of strength, dignity and love for her husband and family. There have been many times when I have gone to that passage to gain strength and wisdom for my life. Here are some things you can do to be an excellent wife. It's not so complicated, but consistency helps.

- Pray for him daily.
- Encourage him in his work.
- Lift him up in other people's eyes.
- Give him physical contact frequently.
- When he leads, follow him.
- When he's wrong, advise him without nagging or whining. When he doesn't change his mind and do things your way, follow him anyway (unless what he is proposing is illegal, immoral or dangerous, of course).
- In marriage, one of the best ways to deal with conflict and with awkward moments during sexual intimacy is to *laugh*! Laughing together—whether it's when you're in conflict and one of

you says something kind of silly or if you just conked him in the nose with an elbow in bed—is a soothing balm that just makes everything better.

Conclusion

The honeymoon is an important transition time from your life as a single, unmarried woman to that of wife. What a wonderful rite of passage this is! One wise wife had this bit of wisdom to pass down to you: "Figure out what your spouse needs and give that to him. What you want and what he wants are not necessarily the same thing!"

Isn't that really the essence of marriage itself?

For Thought and Prayer

1. Talk to your future husband about your expectations for sex on your wedding night and on your honeymoon. Agree to take the pressure for sexual performance off of the wedding night and just enjoy each other physically. Make sure you both have realistic expectations for each other.

2. Discuss your priorities regarding each other and your relationships with your parents. Decide what the ground rules will be for communication, visits and money regarding the in-laws. Agree to always put each other first above your parents and other friends or family members.

3. How and when do you plan to implement each of these decisions?

Resources

You may want to look at these books, especially if you are a virgin. Even if you are sexually experienced, you may want to identify some sections in one of the books to read together with your fiancé this week.

Cutrer, William, and Sandra Glahn. *Sexual Intimacy in Marriage.* Grand Rapids, MI: Kregel Publications, 2001 (especially chapter 6, "The Wedding Night and Beyond," pp. 52-60).

McBurney, Louis, and Melissa McBurney. *Real Questions: Real Answers About Sex.* Grand Rapids, MI: Zondervan Publishing House, 2005 (especially chapter 3, "First Encounter: Expectations and Preparations," pp. 44-58).

Wheat, Ed, and Gaye Wheat. *Intended for Pleasure: Sex Technique and Sexual Fulfillment in Christian Marriage,* 3rd ed. Grand Rapids, MI: Revell Books, 1997.

Chapter Nine

FOR THE GROOM'S EYES ONLY

Then the Lord God made a woman from the rib and brought her to
Adam. "At last!" Adam exclaimed. "She is part of my own flesh and
bone! She will be called 'woman,' because she was taken out of a man."

GENESIS 2:22-23, *NLT*

If you think about it, in this verse Moses records about when Adam
sees his wife, it is not only for the first time but also *without* clothes!
Don't the first words out of Adam's mouth sound funny? I mean,
imagine you're on your honeymoon and you see the splendor of your
new bride without the embellishment of any clothing—would you ever
say, "part of my own flesh and bone"? Well, maybe you should!

Let me illustrate what Adam may have actually been saying by sharing a modern-day version of this exact same emotion.

Betsy told me about her most special honeymoon memory: "I was
really nervous about my husband seeing me (without clothes) for the
first time, because I was self-conscious about my unsightly scars from
past surgeries. When my husband saw me the first time, he had the
greatest response. He said, 'Wow!'" Betsy's eyes misted up as she went
on, her words spilling softly over quivering lips, "*Every* woman should
be told she is that beautiful to her lover's eyes on her wedding night. It
lays a great foundation for the future!"

What a great story! This man, like Adam, gave his new wife a fantastic gift. And, in Betsy's case, he gave her a most cherished memory—
by simply mimicking what Adam did when he first saw Eve.

For those of us not familiar with Hebrew, Adam's words when he
first saw Eve have been translated a variety of ways: "At last!" (*NLT*) or

"This is at last!" (*ESV, NRSV*) or "This one, at last" (*CSB*) or "This is now!" (*NIV, NASB, KJV, ASV*) or "Finally!" (*THE MESSAGE*) or "This is it!" (*TLB*).

But, I think Betsy's husband's "Wow!" may be as good a translation as any. In fact, here's how I'd translate the emotion of Adam's words in Genesis 2:23:

> Wow! My, oh my, oh my! Right in the nick of time! This feminine, sexy work of art is awesome!! This special one is my other, to be part of me, to complete me. Strong where I am weak, weak where I am strong. My match. My perfect match! This masterpiece indeed completes me.

The picture in Genesis is that God uniquely fashioned and then presented the woman to the man (the Hebrew word used here for man is *adam*). Adam sees his wife, in all of her splendor, and in the process becomes, if you would, a new man, as Moses now uses a *different* Hebrew word, *iysh*, to describe Adam. As a single, unmarried man, he was *adam*, and now as a husband, he is *iysh*.

This language change is, I think, sensational. Until this moment in the creation story, the man, the *adam*, had been alone and incomplete.

Then, when he and Eve marry, they not only become one flesh, but also he is assigned a new role, the *iysh*, a term describing the man with very particular God-assigned responsibilities. He is now bestowed the role of husband and must serve as the partner, protector, provider, prophet and priest for what was fashioned and designed to be his most valuable and honored and precious soul mate and companion—his match—his woman—called in Hebrew, *ishshah*.

The word for man as husband, *iysh*, used here in Scripture for the first time is derived from the word *enosh*, which means to march ahead or to lead another in order to blaze a trail into the unknown. The word used by the Scripture for the woman as wife is *ishshah*, which implies a delicate and elegantly crafted and fashioned person of great value and preciousness—and designed to be one with her *iysh*.

Although your role as your new wife's partner, protector, provider, prophet and priest legally and spiritually begins when you are, in your wedding ceremony, declared man and wife (and you sign the wedding license), your first opportunity to vividly and intimately demonstrate to her your desire and willingness to provide this form of servant leadership will be on your wedding night and the subsequent honeymoon.

"How can I do this?" you say. I'm glad you asked! Although there is a lot I want to discuss with you about this topic, let's start with sex.

Starting with Sex

Why start with sex? Because it's likely all you're thinking about when you imagine your wedding night, right?!

A good friend, Andy Braner, teaches hundreds of teens each summer at Kanakuk Colorado, a Christian camp he directs deep in the Rocky Mountains. Of all the talks he gives to kids, one of my favorites is when he teaches them about sexual purity. As part of the lesson, he'll have the girls sit on one side of the auditorium and the boys on the other.

He'll explain that he wants them to raise their hands to indicate yes. Then, he'll ask the girls, "Ever since you were a little girl and you dreamed about your wedding, did you think about your wedding dress?" Virtually all of the girls will laugh and raise their hands. The boys don't move. "How about your attendants? Have you thought about how many you'll have? Who they will be?" Once again, most all of the girls will giggle and raise their hands. The boys begin to look bored. "How about how many guests you'll invite? The wedding cake? The type of ceremony and the type of reception?" Again, virtually all of the girls' hands are in the air and most of the boys are yawning.

"And," Andy inquires, "when you dream about your wedding night, have you fantasized about how you'll enter the room and what you'll wear to bed?" By now all of the girls' hands are up waving and the boys are looking at each other in disbelief.

Then Andy pops *the* question, "And, when you dream and fantasize about your wedding, how many of you think that sex is the most important thing?" The girls' hands drop like rocks.

Andy turns to the boys, now suddenly alert and highly interested, and asks them the same question. They react with unanimously raised hands and hoorays! Finally, they've come awake!

The principle couldn't be clearer! Weddings, wedding nights and honeymoons mean *very* different things to men than they do to women. How you approach your wedding night and honeymoon will be important to the foundation of your marriage; it will be crucial to your new wife's heart, soul and spirit, to her emotional health and to your and her relational and spiritual health—for the rest of your marriage.

It is hoped that you've formed the frame for this foundation by staying sexually pure during your courtship and engagement! It is also hoped that you've added the marriage insurance of using a premarital inventory, participating in premarital counseling *and* have been meeting with a mentor couple. So now, let's pour and set the foundational concrete on which your marriage will ultimately build or crumble. Or as Jesus taught:

> These words I speak to you are not mere additions to your life, homeowner improvements to your standard of living. They are foundation words, words to build a life on. If you work the words into your life, you are like a smart carpenter who dug deep and laid the foundation of his house on bedrock. When the river burst its banks and crashed against the house, nothing could shake it; it was built to last. But if you just use my words in Bible studies and don't work them into your life, you are like a dumb carpenter who built a house but skipped the foundation. When the swollen river came crashing in, it collapsed like a house of cards. It was a total loss (Luke 6:47-49, *THE MESSAGE*).

Does this knowledge about God's view of your role as husband add to the apprehension you were already feeling about the honeymoon? For those of you wise enough to enter your wedding night as virgins (and there are more and more of you as each year goes by), you're probably feeling even more apprehension about what will happen on your wedding night.

Well, relax, and let's spend some time looking at my tips and advice that I believe will help things go smoothly.

Dispelling the Myths

My friend, physician and psychiatrist Louis McBurney MD, and his wife, Melissa, have written a "Real Sex" column for *Christianity Today* magazine's website for some time—and they've written an excellent book: *Real Questions: Real Answers About Sex.* The McBurneys list seven myths that many of their counselees believe:

1. *You'll know what to do by instinct.* You won't! As I've discussed, lovemaking takes some wise instruction and lots of practice.

2. *If you love each other, sex will automatically be great.* Not necessarily! There's *nothing* automatic about romance, timing, arousal, gentleness, closeness and love.

3. *You don't have to be married to enjoy sex to the fullest.* Wrong! The key here is the word "fullest." Any animal can have an orgasm, but something much deeper happens in marital sex.

4. *Sex will be the best thing you've ever experienced.* Ain't so! In fact, for many of the couples I surveyed, the first time they had sex was less that the best. You need to understand and be prepared for the fact that your first marital sex may be a bit disappointing. The McBurneys point out, "Sex isn't on the same scale as the birth of a child, coming together after an absence, walking through a tragic event together." Don't get me wrong, it can be great—but there's much more in your married life that will be much greater.

5. *The more you know about sex, the more you'll want it.* Incorrect! The best sex is dressed in trust and commitment. The McBurneys write, "When you have both an understanding of sex and a commitment to your spouse, desire will grow."

6. *The more partners you have, the better you'll get at making love.* Erroneous!—as I've already discussed.

7. *It's best to find out if you're sexually compatible before committing to marriage.* Not so! The McBurneys rightly teach, "Real sexual compatibility is a response to a deepening relationship, not the prelude to it."[1]

If you have any hang-ups about any of these issues, let me encourage you to deal with them this week. Yes, *this* week—before you leave on your honeymoon. Your premarital counselor, mentor couple or pastor could help you with these issues.

Setting the Table:
A Week or More Ahead of the Wedding

Create a Team of Intercessors

I believe that part of your role as your wife's protector is to recruit a team of men and women who are willing to pray for you during your engagement, your wedding ceremony and your honeymoon.

Morgan Snyder, a friend who serves with Ransomed Hearts Ministry, writes:

> Intentionally, have a team of intercessors for the wedding day and through the night and honeymoon. Despite all the stress and anxiety that surrounds a woman during her wedding, wedding night and honeymoon, our wedding was the single most peaceful, anxiety free day of her life until then, and the honeymoon followed suit. I attribute it almost entirely to the team of friends who very intentionally committed to praying a covering of God's supernatural favor over that time.[2]

Make a Date to Discuss the Wedding Night

As we've discussed earlier, your most important sex organ is your brain. And intercourse means, and starts with, talking—with discussion. So the foreplay for the honeymoon can actually begin *this* week.

When it comes to preparing for your wedding night, I actually recommend that you and your fiancé begin the foreplay *now*, by taking some time *before* the wedding and *before* the wedding night to have a private discussion of your and her expectations for this special night.

Since you and she will *both* remember your wedding night, for better or worse, for the rest of your life, you need to make every effort to make it exceptionally romantic and special.

Before I talk about sex, let's talk a minute about a neat tip my grandfather taught me: He called it mental pictures. It's a simple thing to do. Whenever you and your wife want to remember a particular moment, you take a mental picture together.

First, you develop a silent signal between each other. Second, spend a few seconds soaking in the scene—its smell and feel—the scenery, the temperature, the wind. Then, at some arranged signal—perhaps a hand squeeze or a particular sound—take a mental picture together.

You can even experiment with this during the date. You will be surprised how easy it is to remember these pictures for decades. I have several mental pictures from my wedding. I have one of when the door of the church opened and there Barb stood in her dress, with her dad. The photographer missed that one—but not me!

I have another picture of our standing at the altar, her bouquet shaking from her nervous tremor as a friend played a guitar solo. No way could the photographer have caught that moment—or the sounds or my and her feelings.

After 34 years of marriage, Barb and I still share these mental photos with each other and our children, each wedding anniversary. And we're thankful to my grandfather for teaching us this neat technique.

Well, back to the honeymoon preparation. Whenever Barb and I counsel couples before marriage, we usually find that the man and the woman will have very different expectations of the honeymoon. This is normal. After all, as we've explained, men and women are designed and wired quite differently.

Most men in my survey say they want to have a really, really good sexual time on their honeymoon—preferably starting as soon as possible! Some guys even believe their ideal honeymoon would be to be locked in a plush bedroom with their bride for a whole week—with nothing but athletic and brusque sex, sex, sex—*and* then watch Sports-Center or ESPN on the tube during the rare times of rest!

Most women, on the other hand, imagine a honeymoon with *some* soft, gentle romantic sex—and, even more so, dreamy walks, sunsets, naps and romantic talks scattered among frequent times of rest! They want to walk on the beach holding hands and look at the moon. They desire quixotic candlelit dinners. They imagine dancing around a room in your arms. They view the honeymoon not as a sexual Olympics but as a wonderful, restful, fantastic and romantic time.

So you can see that it's critical to understand your and your wife's expectations of the honeymoon. Once you two have fully discussed your likely different expectations, then *you* can begin to adjust *your* expectations to match hers as closely as possible before the event.

Another assignment I often give the guys I counsel before marriage is to use their honeymoon expectations discussion to begin talking about their future sex life together.

That's what I'd like you to do. During this date, ask your fiancé questions such as

- How are you feeling about our wedding night?
- Are you feeling a bit nervous about our first night as a married couple?
- Are you worried about anything?
- When you think about our wedding night, what comes to mind? What wishes do you have?
- As you imagine our honeymoon, what would make it perfect for you?

Chances are that she will be incredibly relieved to have the opportunity to talk about the subject. Be prepared to listen to her—*really* listen. And be ready to share your hopes and fears.

When your discussion-about-the-wedding-night date begins, here's another recommendation to consider: Each of you take a few minutes to write down all the things that you want out of sex for your marriage. When done, share and discuss each of your lists. What matches? What doesn't?

This is also an ideal time to chat about what psychologists call the misunderstood words of sexual talk—such as the words you will each use to describe your and your spouse's genitals and other body parts. I'd also recommend that you discuss the words or phrases you plan to ask for or describe sex—what phrases or code words you'd like to use. Discuss which terms, phrases or words you both will agree that you find sexy—and, more important, decide which words you will not use if one or both of you find them objectionable or offensive.

Another item I recommend that you discuss, especially if one or both of you are virgins, are the very common questions of (1) Will I be any good at sex? and (2) Will I be able to please my new spouse sexually?

I think it's critical that she know (and knows that you know) that sex, like most things, takes lots of practice. *Every* person feels a little clumsy when first learning how to have sex. Let her know that you plan to take things slowly, talk and listen a lot, and are prepared to laugh together. Let her know that wedding nights are perfect only in the movies and romance novels. So take the pressure off. It will be a great relief to both of you.

One young friend wrote to me, "I sensed God leading me to use my strength for my bride to relieve all 'pressure' or 'expectation,' self-imposed, culturally imposed or otherwise. I shared with her that we had an entire lifetime of intimacy to look forward to and it could only get better because, of course, with all great things there is a learning curve. So I shared with her that my posture was that we had no pressure or obligation even to have sex that first night, as we had a lifetime. And after an incredibly emotional day of marriage, we had an entire week of honeymoon to enjoy that. So we prayed to that end."

How did this approach work out? My young friend explains, "It was huge to break down all preconceptions, pressure, expectations and to make my number-one goal for the night for her to have the emotional and spiritual experience of being at rest, being safe, being delighted and enjoyed."

I couldn't agree more. I think it's important that you let her know that you know how tired and stressed she's going to be that day. Let her know that your goal for your wedding night is to serve and please her—and if that means no sex that night, that's fine with you.

Does this shock you? It shouldn't! I'll explain more about this later in the chapter, but for now, let me tell you a story. Mark, a guy I was counseling, called me up after he and his fiancée, Kathy, shared this date together: "Walt, when I got to the part about not pushing the sex, that I just wanted to be with her and in her arms, to snuggle and talk about the wedding, and if she was exhausted, to just get a great night's sleep, you should have seen her face! She just exhaled and relaxed all over. She got tears in her eyes and reached out and took my hand and told me I had just given her the best wedding present possible. I didn't know how many of her friends had told her how horrible their new husbands were, forcing sex on the wedding night. I'm so glad I knew to have this talk. Thanks!"

If for any reason the subject of your honeymoon in general, or sex in particular, is too uncomfortable for her to discuss with you, be absolutely sure to visit your premarital counselor and mentor couple *before* the wedding. Despite the busyness of the week, it's much, much easier to deal with these issues before, and not on, the honeymoon.

Knowing *her* needs, worries, fears and expectations can allow you to make plans to make the honeymoon even more memorable, romantic and special.

Write a Love Letter

You'll see a trend in my advice. I'm helping you prepare your most important sexual organ—your brain—for the honeymoon.

There is a four-letter word for sexual intimacy that is critical, especially for men, to understand: T-A-L-K. The *Merriam-Webster Dictionary* gives three definitions for the word "intercourse." The first is "connection or dealings between persons or groups." The second, like unto it, is "exchange especially of thoughts or feelings: communion." It's only the third definition that resonates with what was likely on your mind: "physical sexual contact between individuals that involves the genitalia of at least one person."[3]

So to that end, take some time before your wedding and write a love letter to your future spouse for you to read to her on your wedding night. What do you love most about her? What do you find most physically attractive about her? What characteristics do you most admire? How do you feel about being married to her? Are there any significant Scriptures you would like to include?

After getting your letter in shape, maybe taking several drafts before it's ready, write your final letter in your own handwriting to your new bride. Fold and seal your love letter and pack it in your Honeymoon Kit to read to her on your honeymoon.

Plan to Prepare Your Wedding-Night Room

I was terrifically honored to be asked by my son, Scott, to help him prepare his and Jennifer's wedding-night suite. He had arranged with the manager of the hotel to check in the hotel the morning of their wedding. We went up to the honeymoon suite together. I watched with much pride as my son placed Jennifer's favorite comforter on the bed. Then he fluffed and set her favorite pillows and teddy bear at the head of the bed. He had learned how special these were to her and had arranged with her mom to pick them up the morning of the wedding—without Jennifer being aware he had done so.

Then we sprinkled rose petals across the bed. Scott placed votive candles around the bedroom and bathroom. He also set up a small portable sound system with some of their favorite romantic music.

It was a wonderful treat for me to see my son trying so hard to be sensitive to his soul mate and working to make their wedding-night suite a special and comfortable place.

There are many other things you can do to make your wedding night memorable. For example, pack a surprise to delight your new spouse. It doesn't need to be grand or expensive. After all, after the expense and stress of the wedding, this evening is truly an opportunity to reveal that you understand it is the thought that counts.

Here are a few ideas for "bliss on the pillow":

- A romantic card with a handwritten note thanking your wife for everything she did to make your wedding a success and for bringing you so much happiness
- A love poem reminding her of all of the characteristics of her that you esteem and admire

- Letting her read your handwritten letter to her (or reading it to her)
- A single rose, a couple of chocolate truffles and a bottle of champagne (or a bubbly nonalcoholic celebration beverage)—you can usually arrange for the hotel to supply these
- A flower or a bouquet (the hotel can help you arrange this also)
- An inscribed devotional book or book of prayers to share together during your honeymoon
- An inscribed book of poetry or inspirational devotions to read together during your honeymoon

Now, I know that not everyone can do this ahead of time. But knowing what to bring to convert your wedding-night bedroom into *her* room on that night is an investment that will pay dividends for decades to come.

The Night Before the Wedding

The Rehearsal Dinner

The planning of the rehearsal dinner (or luncheon) is usually your or your parents' responsibility. And this is an excellent opportunity for you (and your groomsmen) to honor and esteem your fiancée.

This is *not* the place for bar or barn humor. This is *not* the event for crass skits, unseemly pictures, seedy videos or sordid speeches. And to a great degree, *you* can control this. Let your parents, your best man and groomsmen know, in no uncertain terms, of your desire to be honored yourself and to respect and admire your fiancée.

The Bachelor Party

When I survey men about mistakes they've made during their courtship, wedding or honeymoon and ask them about the one thing they wish they could do again, one of the most common wishes is to have had a different type of bachelor party. Unfortunately, many best men seem to believe the raunchier the bachelor party, the better.

Yet too much partying and the wrong type of partying leaves just about everyone at the bachelor party feeling bad physically, emotionally and spiritually.

Because it's *your* bachelor party (even if your best man is in charge), be sure to let him know that you'd like a party that will leave you and the other men feeling encouraged and edified. Let him know that you want to get plenty of rest the night before your wedding. And let him know to use these eternal principles in his planning:

> Let there be no sex sin or impurity among you. Let no one be able to accuse you of any such things. Dirty stories, foul talk, and coarse jokes—these are not for you. Instead, remind each other of God's goodness, and be thankful. So be careful how you act; don't be fools; be wise. Don't act thoughtlessly. Don't drink too much wine; be filled instead with the Holy Spirit and controlled by Him. Talk with each other much about the Lord, quoting psalms and hymns and singing sacred songs, making music in your hearts to the Lord. Give thanks for everything to our God and Father in the name of our Lord Jesus Christ (Eph. 5:3,15-20, *TLB*).

'Nuff said!

At the Wedding

I advise the men I counsel to consider using the wedding ceremony and reception as a time to flirt with your new wife. Remember that your wedding is not an event in which you are responsible to make every attendee feel comfortable, welcome or special. This is your and your bride's day, not theirs. If you don't speak to everyone who attends, that's fine. But if you don't make special moments for your special woman during the wedding, you're missing the opportunity of a lifetime. Far too many young couples spend far too much time greeting every Aunt Maude and Cousin Jim—not to mention a million other details. You don't need to—and you should not.

Don't forget that your new job as your *ishshah*'s new *tysh* is to concentrate on her. During the ceremony and reception, stop from time to time to whisper a special word into her ear—stop just to stare into her eyes for a moment—stop to share a gentle kiss—stop to flirt with her.

During Scott and Jennifer's wedding, after lighting their unity candle, a solo was sung. Rather than turning and facing the soloist, Scott turned to Jennifer. They had a few moments of private words and a special prayer. It was a wonderful way for Scott to honor and esteem his soul mate—and to share some precious and private moments with her.

Another wise move on Scott's part occurred just after the wedding ceremony. Barb and I were the last of the wedding party to leave the sanctuary. As we reached the door, Scott and Jennifer met us and escorted us and the entire wedding party into a private side room. After we entered, Scott closed and locked the door behind us. The room was a small parlor. He and Jennifer sat on a love seat and Scott announced, "As my first act as Jennifer's husband, I wanted us to share communion with each of you." Then the wedding party shared a brief communion service and time of prayer. Can you imagine the message that gave to Jennifer? I don't know if I've ever been prouder of my son than at that moment.

Travel to the Wedding Chamber

Once you leave the reception, most newlyweds will be heading to the wedding chamber. For some, like our son Scott, it was just a short car ride to the hotel. For others, it may be an hour or two drive. Either way, use this time to let your bride debrief. Give her time to talk. Ask *lots* of questions. Listen, listen, listen.

Share with each other your special memories. Laugh together about special, humorous moments. Don't necessarily worry about getting to the hotel immediately after the ceremony. Most couples do not have a chance to eat very much before their wedding ceremony or at the reception, so don't hesitate to plan a meal. Make reservations for a candlelight dinner at a romantic restaurant near the hotel or in the hotel.

Serving the Plates:
After the Wedding

When You Arrive

When you arrive at the location of your wedding night, and if your luggage is in your car, leave it there. You can come back and get it later (or if there are bell services where you are staying, use them!).

If you are checking in to a hotel, be sure to let them know (if they don't say anything) that it's your honeymoon night. You'll have probably already made all of the arrangements with the manager or the events coordinator, but be sure to remind the front desk.

Like some guys, you may want to have a flower and a handwritten love note waiting at the front desk that the staff will present to your wife. Have her read the note. It should only have a couple of romantic sentences that are about *her*—*not* sex!

If you've been wise and have discussed her expectations ahead of time, you'll know if your new wife wants to be carried across the threshold or not. If so, by all means, do so! Don't worry if it looks or feels dorky or awkward. It will be a memory for a lifetime.

And, if there's any way for your wedding photographer to be there (if your wedding night is in or close to the location at which you are getting married), do so. If not, arrange to have a hotel staff person photograph you as you enter your suite. After the photos, you two will be alone.

If the luggage is still in the car, *you* can go get it and allow her a few moments to get comfortable in her nest.

As one wise groom wrote, "Do *not*, under any circumstances, turn on the television (especially SportsCenter or ESPN)."[4]

First Things First

Once you two are alone, it's not time for you to get what you want. Rather, now it's time for you to serve her—to give her what *she* needs.

Probably the only thing on your mind now is *sex, sex, sex*, right? After all, that's the "main course," correct? That's what this marriage stuff is all about, right?

Ah-hem. Not quite.

If you are going to be her servant leader—if you are going to love her as your own body—then you need to realize that your bride has just survived one of the most stress-filled events of her life. Your goal is sex. Hers is likely to be rest, sleep or even to become unconscious. You're thinking fireworks and sexual bliss. She may be thinking coma.

If either you or your bride is too tired for sexual foreplay, I can guarantee you that sex is not going to be so great. You'd be wiser to give it a rest—even until the next morning. Most couples are shocked to find themselves either totally exhausted from the wedding or totally wired. And I can guarantee you that neither are the best state of mind for sex. So, my man, your job is to take the pressure off of her and yourself.

Be aware that you'll never have this honeymoon time again, so take it *slow* and have fun! She may want to shower alone and change into more comfortable clothes. If so, let her!

By the way, even if you usually sleep in a T-shirt or naked, consider wearing something special on this night. For most women, a man is made more sexual and sensual not by what she sees but by what she hears and imagines.

Set the stage for your marriage carefully. Light some candles; put on some favorite music. Present a small wedding-night gift to her. Consider sharing a time of spiritual bonding consistent with your faith, such as communion or prayer.

She may need to lie down and rest. If so, let her! If you get back to the room with the luggage or take a shower and enter the bedroom ready to go and find her in deep hibernation, do *not* attempt to wake her. If one of you falls asleep or isn't in the mood, that's not abnormal—it's actually more common than you might imagine. And it's certainly *not* a prediction of a doomed marriage.

She may want to just spend the time relaxing and remembering how wonderful your wedding day was. Just do it!

If you possess the self-control and wisdom to let her rest and relax—even get a good night's rest—then when she finally is relaxed or finally awakens, it's far more likely to be heavenly.

She may need just to talk. If so, sit and talk! Consider a meal together. Order room service. Remember, take it slow and have fun.

And after the food and drink arrive, slip the Do Not Disturb sign on your door.

Share with each other the high points of the wedding and what you remember most. Spend some time relaxing, talking about the wedding and about your love for each other. Let things get romantic and sappy. Then the sex that follows will be far more intimate and memorable.

Dr. David Hager, a physician I admire and have worked with for many years, advises the newlywed couple "to spend some time just reflecting on the day of the wedding; to talk again about their commitment to one another and their families; for him to affirm that she is so much more than a physical body to him and reaffirm for her all the reasons that he loves her; to offer to wash her feet as a symbol of his commitment and devotion to her. I believe that a woman needs to know that a lot has gone into making this a special experience."[5]

As I mentioned earlier, Barb and I spent our first four nights as husband and wife in our first apartment. After we arrived, Barb wanted to shower, *alone*. As she did, I put on some soft music and lit the candles.

When she came out of the shower, we sat on the couch and reminisced about the day. I had set up a small altar with a candle, a small silver saucer with some bread and a small silver chalice with some grape juice. I had prepared this without Barb's knowledge. Then we shared our first communion together as a couple. It was an incredibly special time.

The Main Course:
The Wedding Night

Concentrate on Her
At some point, she'll be ready for sex.

For one couple we know of, who chose to drive several hours to their honeymoon hotel, the talking in the car led to touching, and before they knew it, they had consummated their marriage at an Interstate rest stop. For them it was fun and exciting and romantic, and they still laugh when they think about it.

Another couple we know went to bed the night of their wedding. They held each other and talked and laughed and hugged. Finally, Catherine fell asleep in Antonio's arms. He knew the wedding was very stressful for her. At the nighttime reception, he could tell she was running out of steam. By the time they arrived at the hotel room, she was totally exhausted. After they showered, brushed their teeth and put on their bed clothes, neither had the energy to hold their heads up, much less anything else! So, Antonio gave her a back massage and she quickly fell into a deep sleep. He told me, "I smiled at the opportunity to truly love her by being willing to wait. I prayed over her and then quickly fell asleep myself." The next morning, his vibrant, rested, relaxed and ready bride woke him up with a soft whisper in his ear, "Why don't you go brush your teeth. It's time!"

Sex Itself

Remember that when it comes to sexual response, we guys are the microwave ovens of the sex world. We can be ready in an instant and "cook dinner" in a minute.

Women are wired *completely* differently. Sexually, they are Crock-Pots—slow to warm up and slow to simmer. But when they are ready, the meal is divine indeed! So when it comes to the marriage bed, don't skip the foreplay!

Rather than rushing into anything, see if you can slow down time. You may be raring to go, but understand that it physically takes her body longer than yours to become aroused. Think of creating a dream-like state. Really concentrate on the sensuality of this time together. Use soft words and slow, soft touches and soft kisses.

However, let me give you a warning. For some men, especially virgins, the pressure of the wedding can be too much and result in two very, very common first-timer sexual dysfunctions. If you find that being in bed with your new wife finds your penis soft and not "working," absolutely do *not* sweat it. Try to change up the mood. Spend some time kissing and fondling each other. Perhaps make a game out of how many different body parts you can kiss. Let her massage you. You can suggest she take a small dab of K-Y Warming Liquid lubricant and give your genitals a massage.

Second, and much more common, many men can actually have premature ejaculation—even before vaginal penetration. If you sense yourself getting too hot or too worked up too early, slow things down! You'll have *no* trouble "reactivating" after a bit of rest. In fact, slowing things down can increase your orgasm when it comes.

However, if you do orgasm prematurely, it does *not* mean that sex is over. You still need to think of her and how you can please her. Slow and gentle massage of her clitoris can often help her have an orgasm. And she can show you where and how to touch her. Make this a fun time!

Also, use this time to "wow" her. Remember the story of Betsy? Understand that many women are extremely self-conscious about their bodies. Whatever you do, don't criticize or comment negatively about *any* part of your wife's body. She's God's gift to you—as she is! Don't demean her figure or the size of her breasts. Enjoy the gift of her body with your eyes and hands. Use this moment to revel in her. Let her know how fantastic she looks and feels to you. In other words, you cannot say "Wow!" enough.

Talk and touch. Go slow. Caress her slowly, beginning perhaps with a nongenital massage. Work toward her erotic areas slowly; she'll indicate when she's ready for things to heat up. As you do, be prepared to communicate and softly laugh together. Find out what feels good—and what doesn't. Don't be afraid to ask! Try to be gentle with her and focus on how amazing it is to finally be in her arms as her husband. Savor each moment.

Again don't rush things. Start with a massage, perhaps. Some women love to have their nipples stroked or sucked; others don't. Find out where she likes to be touched—and don't frustrate her by doing something that doesn't please her.

Remember that you will be sexually ready in an instant, but she will and should take time. Give her the gift of time. Dr. McBurney writes, "She may be nervous about intercourse. That can cause tension in her pelvic muscles, tightening her vaginal walls and making entrance difficult. An overeager groom only complicates matters by failing to take time with foreplay, arousal and clitoral stimulation."[6]

But finally, when the Crock-Pot is simmering, when she's ready, she'll let you know. Slow foreplay allows her natural lubricants to build up around the labia and in the vagina. Nevertheless, I recommend that if your wife is a virgin, that you *not* attempt intercourse the first time without lubrication. Doing so can increase the risk for irritation of your penis (which will be *no* fun later in the week) and increase the risk of her bleeding or having a painful spasm of her vagina (which can also decrease her sexual desire during the week).

If she's a virgin, I recommend that you let her be in control. One of the most effective ways to do this is to let *her* be on top. You can lie on your back and let her straddle you. This allows you to see her and drink in how great she looks. Be sure to let her know! This position allows you to *gently* feel, touch and massage her breasts. Be sure this is good for her. She can lean forward and kiss you or allow you to kiss her breasts.

This position will allow her to gently move her genitals across yours. Let *her* be in charge of the pace. And when she's ready, let her place your penis inside her. Again, let her control the depth and speed of penetration. If it's uncomfortable for her, then *she* can slow things down. Then once she's let you in, fully in, *slowly* begin to enjoy being truly one.

If at all possible, see to it that she orgasms before you do. And if she tells you it's not going to happen that night, accept it. It's not uncommon or abnormal! There will be thousands of tomorrows—or even just a little bit later!

If the sex isn't the greatest thing you have ever experienced, don't fret. Remember, you've got a lifetime to perfect it.

One last note on premature ejaculation: Some grooms, especially virginal grooms, will have trouble with recurrent premature ejaculation. If so, you can reduce this problem by reducing the sensitivity of your penis. There are two effective ways to do this. One is to wear a condom before and during intercourse. A second is to use a topical anesthetic agent such as benzocaine gel. There are a couple of over-the-counter preparations called Mandelay Climax Control Gel and Detane Male Genital Desensitizer Ointment.

You can find these products in the condom section at your pharmacy. And as a warning here—be sure that you use a condom during

intercourse if you use one of these products! You *don't* want to decrease
her sensitivity with the anesthetic gel!

After Sex

To that end, after sex, don't, don't, *don't* just roll over and go to sleep.
Be sure to spend a few moments just enjoying being with each other.
Tell her how much you love her. You may even want to consider having
a small token of affection to give her.

Some couples enjoy sharing a moment of prayer together—thanking
the Lord for the sacrament He's just given you—an outward and visible
sign (becoming one with your wife) of an inward invisible change (of
being one with your Father in heaven).

However, let me share a warning here, offered by one of the men in
our survey who expressed well the thoughts of others: "(Prayer after sex)
may be perfectly all right for some, but I would like to share my experience. I thought it would be a great idea to have prayer together after sex.
After a few nights, my wife shared with me that it was not working for
her. Her point was that it interrupted the 'afterglow' of the experience
for her. Initially, she was hesitant to tell me, but I understood because of
the difference in the way a man and a woman experience the sexual relationship. My fear is that some of the 'Bible thumping' men (no offense
intended) may jump on this and think his wife is not spiritual if she
doesn't go along with it. I do think it is possible to 'overspiritualize' the
physical. I personally think the prayer idea is great but perhaps it would
be good to have that prayer the next day and not right after consummating the relationship."

How do *you* prevent this? How do you know what she'd prefer?
Simply ask her! Put this on the list of questions you discuss when you
have your date to discuss expectations before your wedding.

As romantic as it may seem, don't go to sleep with your new wife's
head resting on your arm or shoulder. A number of new husbands who
have made this mistake have been chagrinned to wake up and find a weak-
ness of their thumb and index finger resulting in difficulty with pincher
movements of the thumb and index fingers. This malady is called honeymoon palsy. It can take days to weeks to go away, so avoid it at all costs.

When You Awaken

First of all, if you have to leave for your honeymoon the next morning (which I think is dumb, dumb, dumb), be sure to arrange a wake-up call. I hope that after having read this book, you won't have to rush away and will be able to enjoy a long night's sleep before beginning your honeymoon trip.

If you do this, then when you do wake up, don't hop out of bed. Have some bedside mints on standby and enjoy being with each other. Consider ordering a breakfast in bed the first morning.

As you head into your first day as newlyweds, remember one final thing: Avoid arguments today at all costs. Remember the old saying, "Do you want to be right or do you want to be happy?" Or how about this one: "Make love, not war!"

What Have We Left Out?

What have we left out of the Honeymoon Kit? Well, Viagra for one—intentionally. Believe us, your wife is not going to want you to go on forever and neither will you. Leave the sexual stimulation drugs at home and concentrate on enjoying each other as you are, unless you have a serious sexual dysfunction issue and you are under a physician's care.

Conclusion

The honeymoon is an important transition time from your life as a single, unmarried man to that of husband. What a wonderful rite of passage this is! I love this sage advice regarding preparation for sex from one of our survey respondents (and I would extend it to the marriage as a whole): "Figure out what your spouse needs and give that to her. What you want and what she wants are not necessarily the same thing!"

Isn't that really the essence of marriage itself?

Finally, if you've been a wise, sensitive and insightful *tysh*, then your honeymoon will be a time for you to build a firm foundation with your *ishshah* that will last for a lifetime.

For Thought and Prayer

1. Talk to your future wife about your and her expectations for your wedding night and on your honeymoon. You need to take the pressure for sexual performance off your and her shoulders for the wedding night and just enjoy each other physically. Make sure you both have realistic expectations for each other.

2. Are you willing to put her wedding-night needs first, above your desires and needs?

3. How and when do you plan to implement each of these decisions?

Resources

You may want to look over one of these books this week, especially if you are a virgin. If you both are virgins, then you may want to identify some sections in one of the books to read together this week. Even if you are sexually experienced, I still strongly suggest picking one of the "sex" books and looking it over. In addition, I recommend you, as the spiritual leader of your marriage, read one of the books about praying as a couple.

"Sex" Books

Cutrer, William, and Sandra Glahn. *Sexual Intimacy in Marriage.* Grand Rapids, MI: Kregel Publications, 2001 (especially chapter 6, "The Wedding Night and Beyond," pp. 52-60).

McBurney, Louis, and Melissa McBurney. *Real Questions: Real Answers About Sex.* Grand Rapids, MI: Zondervan Publishing House, 2005 (especially chapter 3, "First Encounter: Expectations and Preparations," pp. 44-58).

Wheat, Ed, and Gaye Wheat. *Intended for Pleasure: Sex Technique and Sexual Fulfillment in Christian Marriage,* 3rd ed. Grand Rapids, MI: Revell Books, 1997.

"Praying as a Couple" Books

Fuller, Cheri. *When Couples Pray: The Little-Known Secret to Lifelong Happiness in Marriage.* Sisters, OR: Multnomah Publishers, 2001.

Dobson, Jim, and Shirley Dobson. *Night Light: A Devotional for Couples.* Sisters, OR: Multnomah Press, 2000.

Rainey, Dennis. *Two Hearts Praying as One.* Sisters, OR: Multnomah Press, 2000.

Rainey, Dennis, and Barbara Rainey. *Moments Together for Intimacy: Devotions for Drawing Near to God and One Another.* Ventura, CA: Regal Books, 2003.

Stoop, Jan, and David A. Stoop. *When Couples Pray Together: Creating Intimacy and Spiritual Wholeness.* Ann Arbor, MI: Vine Books, 2000.

Part Three

Chapter Ten

DAILY REFLECTIONS FOR THE HONEYMOON

If two of you on earth agree about anything you ask for, it will be done for you by my Father in heaven. For where two or three come together in my name, there am I with them.

MATTHEW 18:19-20

Some of the best marriages we know are those that make a regular habit of sharing not only quality time together as a couple but also quantity time! Using at least some of this time to pray together as a couple can be a powerful influence in building and strengthening a life-long marriage.

Now, we're the first to admit that this can be hard, especially if you are not used to praying out loud or with someone! To make this transition easier for you, we have written this next section of the book to serve as a seven-day starter for beginning as a couple to spend time each day to pray for and journal about your marriage. The following readings are short and to the point but were especially chosen and written as brief topics specifically for the honeymoon week.

We encourage you to begin the lifelong habit of quiet time together during your honeymoon, but consider transitioning to one of many excellent couple's devotionals to continue after your honeymoon. Some of our favorites are

- *Meditations for the Newly Married* by John M. Drescher (Scottsdale, PA: Herald Press, 1986)
- *Moments Together for Intimacy: Devotions for Drawing Near to God and One Another* by Dennis and Barbara Rainey (Ventura, CA: Regal Books, 2003)

- *Night Light: A Devotional for Couples* by Jim and Shirley Dobson (Sisters, OR: Multnomah Press, 2000)
- *Two Hearts Praying as One* by Dennis Rainey (Sisters, OR: Multnomah Press, 2000)

Day 1
New Life, New Beginnings

First day of the marriage of Mr. and Mrs._____

Date:_____

We hope that you have much to be thankful about today as you start your new life together on your honeymoon.

Congratulations, Mr. and Mrs.!

You can probably see now, from your new perspective as husband and wife, that the foundations of your marriage were laid long before you said, "I do." It was, without a doubt, a lot of hard work and preparation to get to this point! We believe that God's hands were on your lives and your hearts before the beginning of time, setting the wheels in motion through your parents, your parent's parents, your faith community, your teachers, your friends and your dreams for each other.

Now breathe a long, deep breath. Can you feel the freshness of your new marriage, the joy in your heart? Remember these feelings. Relive this joy of the next few days again and again. Use your memories and what you have recorded as an anchor for the rest of your marriage.

Choose to set your heart on the purpose for your marriage and your love for each other. Perfection is not found in flawlessness but in growing closer in your marriage and your lives together.

Time Together: Express gratitude to your spouse for your marriage and for each other, listing at least five blessings you've experienced this week. Thank, in prayer and in writing, five individuals who helped you get here today.

Day 2
Your Meals Together

If the foundations for your marriage were set before the history of time, the next step is for you to build on that with the blueprint for your family. Yes, you are a new family now, just the two of you. A family starts with a husband and a wife.

So, where to begin? A great place is by learning to share mealtime together as husband and wife. In our hurried society, one family tradition that has fallen by the wayside in many households is that of a shared mealtime. Mealtimes can be special times to share each other's company, discuss the day's events (past or upcoming), and plan today or the following day. As your family grows, shared meals can become a hub of togetherness, an important gathering time for communication and friendship.

For today, choose a meal to repeat on your anniversary next year. Choose a restaurant with a type of food that you both enjoy or, if your accommodations allow it and you love cooking, cook a special meal together.

Set the table and set a time to eat. Think about what your spouse would like. Make it a special meal today.

Time Together: Make a commitment to schedule at least one meal together each day, despite your busy schedules. If this isn't possible, aim for five meals a week together. Make it a habit. Talk about other times that you would like to commit to setting aside just for each other as you start your married life.

Day 3
New Traditions—Choose a Marker

Markers and traditions are a very important part of family. They are a means of passing down the history of your lives and significant events to your children and future generations. They also serve as reminders of vows and covenants—such as marriage.

For Dale and Sue, a purchase that they made on their honeymoon has become one of those markers. Dale and Sue were married at Christmas time (on December 22). They went to Breckenridge, Colorado, for their honeymoon. While shopping one day, they came across a small store that sold, to the best of their recollection, nothing but nativity scenes, and they bought one made by Goebel (Hummel) that is all white porcelain. Goebel is also significant in Sue's family history, as her family is only second-generation American, with strong German heritage. Sue's grandmother and mother both collected Hummels.

They had the nativity set shipped back home, and it has become a cherished reminder of their honeymoon and a tradition that adds to their family Christmas celebration as a reminder of their ancestors and heritage.

Talk about what you may want to bring home to your new house as a symbol of and reminder of your honeymoon—something that could even become a family heirloom. It doesn't need to be extravagant—in fact, the simpler the better. It doesn't need to cost anything at all. We've known quite a few couples who brought home a newly conceived pregnancy as their little marker . . . *hmmm.*

Time Together: Talk with each other about what you may want to bring home from your honeymoon as a marker or reminder of this special time together.

Day 4
Ground Rules

Okay, we know this is your honeymoon and all, but it's Day 4. By now, a fair percentage of newlyweds have already had their first disagreement and at least one argument. That's not only A-OK, it means you're perfectly normal!

The first fight does not mean your marriage is over! Couples who love each other have civil and mature disagreements, work them out as loving adults and then love each other even more. So it is important to fight fair when you disagree, and in order to do that, we should set some ground rules.

First, don't say things you don't mean, even in anger. Guard your mouth when you speak. Our words have power, and you will be held to what you say.

Along those lines, both Sue and I have a rule in our marriages that has served us well: We will *never* use the *D* word, even in anger. Since we've agreed that divorce will *never* be an option for us, we *never* use the word. To do so would corrode the trust and stability of even the strongest of relationships.

It's okay for you to be irritated at times with one another. That's going to happen. What's really important is how you handle working through these issues and this adjustment phase as you start your life together. In marriage, love is a decision, not an emotion—love is action, not feeling.

Sue has a friend, Jill, who says this: "There have been times when I have been hurt by or have become angry with my husband and I make the decision to love and remember all the things about him that I love. It makes getting over the silly things so much easier."

Don't go to bed angry. Don't let the sun set on your anger. Learn how to say you're sorry. Make up. Forgive each other. Resolve your issues. And then, move forward. That's how a healthy marriage grows.

Time Together: Take a moment of quiet reflection and list the things you especially appreciate about your spouse—especially if he or she has done something to bug you today. Ask forgiveness for your mistakes. Now go kiss and make up.

Day 5
Who Owns It?

Dr. Jim Martin and his wife of more than 35 years, Mignon, are two of Sue's most cherished role models and mentors—not just for marriage, but for life. As director of the CHRISTUS Santa Rosa Family Practice Residency Program, Jim was Sue's boss for almost seven years and her neighbor for three. When it comes to being a great example of friendship and spiritual marriage, the Martins set the bar very high indeed, devoting their lives not only to each other but also to helping and coaching others toward better living and better marriage.

Several years ago, Jim and Mignon came to speak to Sue and Dale's small group about successful marriage and parenting. Among the many important lessons they taught, one of the most surprising and memorable has been this idea concerning marriage: The issue is simply, "Who owns it?"

Who does what? We bet you have found that even five days into your marriage, this issue has presented itself. Who makes the bed, cleans up the trash, cleans up after sex, makes the coffee in the morning and takes responsibility for holding the room key?

At home, the questions might concern who is responsible for paying the bills, making the beds, handling the in-laws, picking up the mail, taking care of the kids and feeding the dog! Who is expected to initiate sex, buy the birth control and make the reservations for date night?

The important issue here is not who does what, but rather what are the "whats," and does each "what" have a "who" assigned to do it?

Organize your family tasks, dividing them up and realizing that this list will need to be revised periodically—after all, life happens. Now take responsibility for your part, remembering that marriage is not 50-50—it's a 100%-100% proposition.

Taking ownership of your tasks doesn't mean you can't ask for help if you need it. It just means you make sure it gets done. Good leadership delegates but does not take advantage of that effort.

Time Together: List the tasks of daily living that need to be done to keep your family functioning. Pledge to devote your hearts to serving each other and taking ownership of your responsibilities.

Day 6
Taking Care of Each Other

Take some time today to journal about your memories of this honeymoon. Remember what it feels like to love and care for each other for the first time as a married couple. Take a memory snapshot of this moment and keep it with you. Multiply that by every day of the rest of your lives together, fed by nurturing and love, and then you are far more likely to be more madly in love when you are much older.

I remember an elderly couple celebrating their sixtieth anniversary, hand in hand, with the sparkle of love still very much alive in their eyes. That sparkle, that light, only comes from a life lived with love, service, patience and practice in taking care of each other. It's a beautiful way to go through marriage.

Time Together: Think about couples you know that have celebrated 25 or more years of marriage together. List some of the characteristics you admire about their marriage. Talk with each other about what you want your marriage to look like when you reach their age. If you don't yet have a mentor couple, talk about who you might approach to ask to be your mentor couple for your first year of marriage.

Day 7
Joy for Each Other and in Each Other

On the seventh day of creation, God rested—and we hope you are doing the same. Can't you just picture God kicking back on the seventh day, feet up, perusing all of creation, pleased with His work and basking in its joy? Then He blessed creation, actually voicing His pleasure at His work.

What are you joyful for today? You are nearing the completion of your honeymoon—the creation and foundation week of the rest of your marriage. Are you resting and reflecting on it with joy? Have you told your spouse how much you love him or her and how happy you are?

We love the example of Solomon, the wisest man ever to live, taken from the Song of Songs in the Bible.

The Man
Dear, dear friend and lover . . . Your beauty is too much for me—I'm in over my head. I'm not used to this! I can't take it in. There's no one like her on earth, never has been, never will be. She's a woman beyond compare. My dove is perfection, pure and innocent as the day she was born, and cradled in joy by her mother. . . . "Has anyone ever seen anything like this—dawn-fresh, moon-lovely, sun-radiant, ravishing as the night sky with its galaxies of stars?"
SONG OF SONGS 6:4,5,8-10, *THE MESSAGE*

The Woman
My dear lover glows with health—red-blooded, radiant! He's one in a million. There's no one quite like him! His eyes are like doves, soft and bright, but deep-set, brimming with meaning, like wells of water. His face is rugged, his beard smells like sage, his voice, his words, warm and reassuring. He stands tall, like a cedar, strong and deep-rooted, a rugged mountain of a man, aromatic with wood and stone. His words are kisses, his kisses words. Everything about him delights me, thrills me through and through! That's my lover, that's my man, dear Jerusalem sisters.
SONG OF SONGS 5:10,12-13,15-16, *THE MESSAGE*

Time Together: Be thankful for joy in your life and your marriage. Be thankful for your spouse's companionship and happiness with you and your marriage. Communicate to your spouse how much he or she means to you and how happy you are. Live joyfully!

CONCLUSION

It has been a total joy for us to write this book for you. Both Sue and I have enjoyed the privilege our patients have given us to care for them, and the feedback they've given us through the years that have helped us develop the ideas we've shared with you. But most of all, we're honored that you've allowed us the pleasure of passing on to you (1) the wisdom of the Bible; (2) the tips and advice of physicians, clergy, counselors and friends we admire; and (3) the feedback of the hundreds of engaged couples for whom we've cared and whose comments and experiences we have given you to consider for your honeymoon.

Will marriage be easy? Of course not!

Will it be worth it? You can't even begin to imagine.

Lyle Dorsett, a theologian and writer I admire, wrote to me about his parents' lifelong honeymoon:

When my father and mother celebrated their fiftieth wedding anniversary, I asked my father to share with me some of the things he had learned in their very good marriage. He said that I needed to know that when he first met my mom he fell in love. And when they got married and went on their honeymoon, he thought they could never be more in love.

Nevertheless, preparing for their honeymoon was his way of preparing "the pot" into which he and my mom would plant their newfound love for a lifetime of growth. And over the years, he saw their true and deep love grow deeper and stronger over time as he and mom grew together through joys, sorrows and problems—through the harvests and droughts of life together.

He told me, "I never had any idea when I married your mother fifty years ago how little I knew about love and how much I would love her in the years ahead."[1]

We pray God's richest blessings upon you, your spouse, the remaining portion of your engagement and courtship, your wedding, your wedding night, your honeymoon, your family and your marriage.

Our goal in writing this book was to introduce you to the divine design for marriage, beginning with your honeymoon, along with our collective experience and advice about planning a honeymoon.

We believe this approach is unique and we hope we've delivered it to you with a different twist than is usual in our society—and that you now see your honeymoon as more than just a fun, sex-filled vacation.

In essence, we want your honeymoon to be the foundation—the launchpad—for a lifelong honeymoon. Your honeymoon should be a time when you focus on each other and begin your adjustment to marriage. We believe that if you follow the divine design, then your honeymoon has the potential to become a honeymoon that lasts a lifetime.

And I pray that Christ will be more and more at home
in your hearts as you trust in him. May your roots go
down deep into the soil of God's marvelous love.

EPHESIANS 3:17, *NLT*

Part Four

Appendix A

HONEYMOON KIT
CHECKLIST

Setting the Mood	Female Health Items
❐ Romantic reading—your love letters to each other, a book of poetry, Song of Solomon, this book, etc.	*Purchase over the counter:*
	❐ Uristat
❐ Small votive candle(s) and candle holder(s)	❐ 1 zip-lock baggie
	❐ 1 small box of baking soda
❐ Matches or a lighter	❐ Monistat or other vaginal yeast medication
❐ Bubble bath or bath oils	
❐ Sweet-smelling body lotion, perfume or massage oils	❐ Tampons and/or pads—just in case
	❐ Mandelay, Detane, or other topical anesthetic gel
❐ Personal lubricant	
❐ Astroglide	*Talk with my doctor and get prescriptions (and fill them) for:*
❐ K-Y Warming Liquid	
	❐ Antibiotic, in case of a bladder infection (generic Macrodantin or Bactrim)
Other things I would like to bring for romance:	
❐ Music/Favorite CD	❐ Birth control prescription
❐ CD Player or Mp3 player	❐ Monilial vaginitis oral medication (i.e., Diflucan)
❐ Food or Snacks	
❐ Glitter lotion	Other prescriptions:
❐ _____	❐ _____
❐ _____	❐ _____
❐ _____	❐ _____

Quick Instructions:

1. One zip-lock bag to fill with ice or cold water to apply as a pack as needed. It's common for women to have some minor swelling and irritation when first sexually active—especially with repeated activity, like on a honeymoon. You may be glad you packed this!

2. Uristat (buy over the counter)—this is a potent urinary tract pain reliever. Follow package instructions. It should not make you sleepy. Do not take if you have sensitivity to the ingredients!

3. Antibiotic, in case of bladder infection. (Ask your doctor for a prescription and instructions. Please make sure you do not take something to which you have a known allergy!) It is normal to have some external irritation or minor abrasions initially with intercourse that can cause some discomfort when urinating. Don't confuse this with an infection!

   Symptoms of a bladder infection would include persistent burning on urination along with one or more of the following:

   (a) crampy bladder pain in the midline of the abdomen just above the pubic bone;
   (b) cloudy urine;
   (c) foul-smelling urine;
   (d) fever not associated with another possible source; or
   (e) back pain (kidney pain) on either side just below the rib cage. If you need to take the antibiotic, follow the directions of your physician or prescription. One thing you can do to help prevent infections is to urinate after intercourse if possible.

4. Acetaminophen (Tylenol), ibuprofen (Advil, Motrin), or naproxen (Aleve, Anaprox, Naprosyn) for just general aches and pains or fever (or that inconvenient headache).

5. Baking soda—the best cure for vaginal irritation or itching is a soothing baking-soda bath. Don't use soap or bubbles—just cover the bottom of the tub with a thin layer of baking soda and have a nice soak in warm water.

6. Any over-the-counter feminine yeast preparation you would like—follow the directions on the package. You shouldn't need to use this unless your husband has a case of jock itch going into the honeymoon! Use only after the baking-soda bath has failed and if you are really going crazy with itching! Do not take if you have sensitivity to the ingredients!

7. Multivitamins—to help you maintain or recover your strength!

HONEYMOON PACKING LIST

First Aid—General Medical

Purchase over the counter:

❒ Antibiotic cream (e.g., Neosporin, Bacitracin or Bactroban)
❒ Anti-allergy tablets (e.g., Claritin, Benadryl)
❒ Anti-diarrheal medication (e.g., Imodium AD)
❒ Antiseptic liquid or lotion
❒ Antacid (e.g., Tums, Maalox, Mylanta)
❒ Band-Aids/bandages
❒ Cold and congestion medicines (e.g., Sudafed or Afrin Nasal Spray)
❒ Cortisone 0.5% or 1% anti-itch cream
❒ Cough syrup and throat lozenges
❒ Eye drops or eye lubricant
❒ DEET-containing insect repellant
❒ Indigestion or heartburn remedies (e.g., Tagamet, Zantac, Pepcid, Prilosec)
❒ Jock itch/athlete's foot crème (e.g., Lamisil Cream, Lotrimin AF)
❒ Lip protection balm or stick (with sunblock)
❒ Moleskin for blisters
❒ Multivitamin (with folic acid)
❒ Pain relievers (e.g., aspirin, acetaminophen, ibuprofen)
❒ Pepto-Bismol tablets (to prevent traveler's diarrhea)
❒ Saline nasal spray
❒ Moisturizing skin lotion or hand cream
❒ Sunscreens with an SPF of 20 or higher
❒ Sunburn products (e.g., aloe vera lotion or sunburn cream)
❒ For cruisers: seasickness acupressure bands or pills

Talk with my doctor and get prescriptions (and fill them) for:

❒ Scopolamine patches (to prevent seasickness, if going on a cruise)
❒ Medication to prevent or treat altitude sickness (e.g., Diamox or dexamethasone)
❒ Prescription for antibiotic for both of you in case of traveler's diarrhea (Flagyl or Cipro)

Other prescriptions or medications:

❒ _____
❒ _____
❒ _____

Long-Distance Honeymoon in the United States or Caribbean

- Have your travel agent shop for the best travel and accommodation packages. Feel free to compare on the Internet, but use the agent. In most cities there are travel agents who specialize in honeymoon travel. I have had couples recommend BeverlyClarkTravel.com as an excellent resource.

- Consider an all-inclusive resort or cruise for simplicity. In general, all-inclusive resorts or cruise packages offer good to great values for honeymooners. However, be sure to examine each carefully to see *exactly* what is included (and excluded) in the price. Be sure to compare your favorite package(s) to a la carte resorts or honeymoons. Nevertheless, all-inclusive packages allow you to know ahead of time exactly what you will spend. All-inclusive resorts also allow active honeymooners the opportunity to try snorkeling, scuba diving, horseback riding, or many, many other new experiences without worrying about extra cost.

- Make flights with the least number of changes. Remember that the earlier in the day you fly, the less likely you are to be canceled and if you are canceled or delayed, the more likely you are to be placed on another flight.

Foreign Travel

We do *not* recommend foreign travel for a honeymoon. True, there are many exotic locations, but virtually every part of the travel is more complex and more likely to be associated with disruption—with the possible exception of popular Canadian or Mexican resorts that cater to Americans. Remember, our key honeymoon travel rule: KISSO (keep it simple, spiritual ones!) But if you do decide to go against our advice:

- Definitely use a travel agent with experience in booking the locale or country to which you are traveling—unless one or both of you is *very* familiar with the location.

- Make sure you know exactly what to expect for accommodations.

- Make sure you know the language or will be able to communicate.

- *Don't* go on a tour.

- Be prepared with

    - Passports or visas. Also, have at least one photocopy of your passport's data page, date and place of issuance, and passport number with a contact person at home. You should also travel with a set of these photocopies in addition to an extra set of loose passport photos for speed in attaining a replacement. Contact the local U.S. Embassy or Consulate immediately if your passport is lost or stolen.
    - Vaccinations as needed. Helpful information on specific locations and general travel can be found at www.cdc.gov/travel/ and www.tripprep.com.
    - Knowledge of the political climate for tourism.
    - Knowledge of how to prevent jet lag (see the section on preventing jet lag in chapter 7).

- Get travel advisory updates 24 hours a day by calling the Department of State's Office of Overseas Citizens' Services at (202) 647-5225.

- Obtain additional, and very helpful, official information for U.S. citizens regarding international travel from www.travel.state.gov.

- Obtain current information regarding the country you will be visiting from foreign embassies and consulates located in the United States.

- Purchase traveler's checks (they are safer than cash); however, we recommend that you try to always use credit cards when traveling internationally. Virtually every country will accept U.S. dollars in tourist areas. Unfortunately, local merchants are often expert at ripping off tourists using unfair exchange values. Major credit card companies, on the other hand, will automatically convert your purchases to U.S. dollars using the correct current conversion on the day of your purchase. You can check with your bank or card company for the details.

- Become familiar with foreign cellular phone(s) and/or e-mail capabilities.

- Use security belts or pouches—these can be important with domestic or Caribbean travel but are even more essential with international travel. These belts are thin and are worn under clothing. They can be fitted snugly around your waist, leg or neck. We recommend you use a security belt to keep your most critical documents and extra cash away from pickpockets. Some companies even make waterproof security pouches that are worn like a fanny pack and can be worn when you snorkel or swim. That keeps important items with you and not foolishly left on the beach. Check out one of our favorite travel stores by searching "money belt":

  - Magellan's—www.Magellans.com
  - Travel Smith—www.travelsmith.com
  - Orvis—www.orvis.com
  - Eagle Creek—www.eaglecreek.com
  - JC Penney Samsonite belt—www.jcpenney.com
  - Amazon—www.amazon.com

- Be sure to get the phone numbers of your traveler check and credit card companies. It will be a different number from their U.S. 1-800 numbers.

- Write down the phone numbers to the local U.S. Embassy or Consulate. We recommend that you contact not only a local tourism bureau for the area into which you will be traveling but also that you contact the U.S. Embassy or Consulate for that region. With assistance from both of these sources you will be able to determine the travel requirements and recommendations for your chosen travel destination. You can get a list at (202) 647-5225 or visit www.travel.state.gov.

- Travel under your maiden name. If you are planning to change your name after you are married, this change may not be reflected on all of your legal documents by the time you are married (i.e., driver's license, passport, airline tickets, etc.—in many states you can't do this until *after* you are married and have a marriage license). Take a copy of your marriage license with you to prove you're married, but as far as reservations, it's usually easier to travel under your maiden name until *all* documents reflect your new married name. With increased travel security both domestically and internationally, security personnel are stricter on people whose names do not match every single travel document and reservation—and in some cases *no* exceptions will be made. When you return from your trip, you can proceed with changing your name on documents with your marriage certificate.

Other Travel Tips

- If you contract for a rental car, consider paying extra for emergency roadside assistance.

- If traveling by air, pay for airline tickets with a credit card, not a check or cash.

- Remember to check in early, even though you may already have boarding passes from your travel agent. Often boarding passes given by the travel agents are different and can delay the check-in process or, worse, delay your entire trip.

- When requesting seat assignments, remember that the seats in the emergency exit row and behind the bulkhead usually have the most leg room. Also, the seats immediately in front of an emergency exit row will not recline (the same is true of the front row if there are two rows of emergency seats together). A seating assignment is not guaranteed. Overweight persons and disabled persons will not be assigned emergency exit row seats.

- Pack light. Most people do not use half of what they pack for their honeymoon. Lugging around a huge suitcase is not romantic and does not allow you to enjoy your trip to its fullest. Choose clothes you can mix and match. No one is going to know (or care) if you've worn the same outfit twice in one week! No matter where you're going or to what climate, always make sure you pack one outfit that can be dressed up, and pack a bathing suit (yes, even if you're going to the North Pole).

- Roll your clothes—don't fold them. Travel professionals tell us this takes up much less space. You can find special bags that compress clothing (like sweaters and other bulky clothes) and press out all the air, thus giving you even more packing space.

- Be sure to attach secure name tags not only on the outside of each piece of your luggage but also on the inside. Make sure the name(s) on your tags match the name(s) on your airline tickets. Another trick is to tuck a copy of your itinerary in with the name tag inside the luggage. This way, if your luggage gets lost, the itinerary can be examined and your luggage will be sent to you wherever you are on your trip.

- Mark your luggage with a bit of wedding ribbon or brightly colored belt or tag. Travel experts say that 90 percent of all travel bags are now black. Do something creative to set your bags apart.

- Do not take anything that's especially valuable. This may include your engagement ring, especially if you have a particularly large diamond and will be traveling in an area where you might be considered a conspicuous target. A plain wedding band will draw less attention. If you must take something of value, be sure it's in your carry-on bag (or worn) and with you at *all* times.

- Take only a small amount of cash (for tips and minor expenses). Otherwise, take most of your money in traveler's checks or credit cards for increased security.

- Be sure to double-check your carry-on bags to be sure there are no items that will cause you to be searched and slowed down at a security point. Pointed scissors (blades longer than 4 inches), lighters and many Leatherman-type tools will be confiscated and will subject you to time-delaying searches. The regulations change as the security risks change, so be sure to check with your airline about the most recent recommendations.

- Be sure that you are not wearing or carrying anything (belt buckle, jewelry, heavy necklace, bracelets, etc.) that might set off a metal detector. If you *must* wear jewelry while flying, bring a small zip-lock baggie in your purse into which you can place your jewelry and place in your purse as you go through security. This will prevent your setting off the metal detector (and can prevent that dropped earring).

- Remember that you'll usually have to remove your shoes and outer coat to go through airport security. Pick shoes that you can easily slip on and off.

- Be sure that *all* the shoes you bring are broken in and comfortable to wear. Many airports require surprisingly long hikes between gates—especially if you're flying internationally. A blister on your foot can make your honeymoon miserable.

- Keep hydrated. It's not at all uncommon for air travelers to become dehydrated while flying, so drink plenty of water during your flight.

- Consider purchasing inflatable pillows, which save room by being collapsible but provide much-needed head and neck support on long flights and journeys.

- If your flight will feature a movie, consider bringing your own small set of earphones (like you'd use with a CD player or Mp3 player). These earphones work on most planes. It can save a rental fee.

- Apply a sunscreen or lotion that has an SPF of 20 or more at least 20 minutes before you go outside. If you'll be sweating or swimming, use a waterproof variety. Reapply the lotion or cream often. You cannot use too much!

- If you are extra sun sensitive, look for any of several varieties of specially designed sun-protection clothing that can block out much of the sun's harmful rays and keep you cool at the same time. Some of these sun-protection clothing items are designed to be worn in the water while swimming or snorkeling. RIT makes a laundry additive called Sun Guard that can be added to cotton clothing to make it sun-protective. This is a less expensive option than some of the clothing you find online. Although it will wear off after 20 washings, you can pick the shirt or pants based on comfort before you treat the fabric. Sun Guard is endorsed by leading dermatologists. It also has received the Skin Cancer Foundation's Seal of Recommendation.

- Pack romantic extras. If your room has a CD or Mp3 player, bring along your favorite romantic songs. Bring your favorite massage oils or lotions, travel candles (yes, they do make them), romantic lingerie and maybe even a little surprise or two to place on your spouse's pillow on your first night together. Be creative and have fun!

Very Important

Consider leaving these items with family, a close friend or your pastor or attorney before you go:

• Photocopy of all travel details (complete itineraries, names, addresses and telephone numbers)

• Photocopies of your passport, credit cards and traveler's check receipts

• A sealed copy of your wills, life insurance policy numbers and pertinent financial information

• Photocopy of credit cards along with 24-hour telephone number to report loss or theft (Call your credit card companies in advance, letting them know where you will be traveling. Credit card fraud detection systems are becoming so sensitive that even irregular shopping habits within your own city might be questioned, let alone charges halfway around the world. Don't risk getting cut off without your credit. Call ahead.)

• Photocopy of traveler's checks along with 24-hour telephone number to report loss or theft

• Any irreplaceable items

Individual Lists

Our list below should only be considered an outline of suggestions. Your list will vary based upon the climate of where you're going and the season. Also, prior to departure you will need to check the specific airline restrictions regarding what items you are not allowed to carry on board.

Although we've created a His and a Her list, you will see many duplicate items. If you plan carefully, you can reduce your luggage weight by combining items. For example, many newlyweds who are used to packing separate toiletry kits can sometimes save space by sharing some items such as toothpaste, shaving cream, floss, deodorant, etc.

Hers

- Carry-on bag—to be kept with you. Pack emergency supplies to carry you through 48 hours in case your checked luggage is lost. Note that specific regulations for carry-on bags can change quickly as the security risks change. Be sure to check with your airline, travel agent or TSA about the most recent recommendations.

  - Honeymoon Kit (see chapters 8 and 9). Some of the items listed in the kit may be restricted, so be sure to check with your airline, travel agent or TSA the week you travel.
  - Makeup, hairbrush, toothbrush and toothpaste may be restricted, so be sure to check ahead
  - One lingerie outfit
  - A change of undergarments
  - One comfortable, versatile, wrinkle-proof outfit—Sue's favorite is a long, black, draping microfiber dress. It is comfortable to travel in, easily washed and goes from airport to shopping to nice restaurant with ease. It can be wadded up in a suitcase and pulled out without ironing. It washes easily in a sink by hand and dries overnight.
  - Snacks and bottled water may be restricted, so be sure to check ahead
  - Wallet, photo ID, passport, driver's license, complete travel itinerary and travel documents
  - Emergency money, traveler's checks and/or credit cards
  - Jewelry and valuables
  - Handiwipes for freshening up may be restricted, so be sure to check ahead
  - All prescription medications in their original bottles

- Suitcase—to be checked through, if flying

  - Travel wardrobe, appropriate for the week's travel activities (casual and dressy clothes)
  - Bedroom wardrobe—remember the adage: For a long and happy marriage, pay as much attention to your bedroom wardrobe as your daytime clothes.
  - Toiletries that are not in your carry-on bag (Remember, your Honeymoon Kit is already with you in your carry-on bag.)

    - Hair dryer, hair spray, shampoo, brush, hair accessories, etc.
    - Toothbrush, toothpaste, floss, mouthwash, mints
    - Makeup
    - Shaving kit

  - Bathing suit and swimsuit cover-up
  - Shoes (dress, sports, sandals—but all should be broken in and comfortable), workout clothes and a pair of water shoes for kayaking or other water sports
  - Hose/undergarments/socks
  - Jacket or coat, sweater(s), scarves

His
- Carry-on—to be kept with you. Pack emergency supplies to carry you through 48 hours in case your checked luggage is lost. Note that specific regulations for carry-on bags can change quickly as the security risks change. Be sure to check with your airline, travel agent or TSA about the most recent recommendations.

  - Honeymoon Kit (see chapters 8 and 9). Some of the items listed in the kit may be restricted, so be sure to check with your airline, travel agent or TSA the week you travel.
  - Brush, comb, toothbrush, toothpaste may be restricted, so be sure to check ahead
  - A change of undergarments

- One comfortable, versatile, wrinkle-proof outfit
- Snacks and bottled water may be restricted, so be sure to check ahead
- Wallet, photo ID, passport, driver's license
- Emergency money, traveler's checks, and/or credit cards
- Jewelry and valuables

- Suitcase—to be checked through, if flying

  - Travel wardrobe, appropriate for the week's travel activities (casual and dressy shirts and pants/shorts)
  - Bedroom attire
  - Toiletries
  - Toothbrush, toothpaste, floss, mouthwash, mints
  - Shaving kit
  - Bathing suit, sunglasses, hat/cap
  - Shoes (dressy, casual, athletic, sandals—but be sure that all pairs are comfortable and broken in), workout clothes and a pair of water shoes for kayaking or other water sports
  - Undergarments/socks
  - Jacket or coat, sweater(s), tie(s), belts—some restaurants require jacket and tie
  - All prescription medications in their original bottles

Other Items to Consider

- Complete travel itinerary and travel documents, auto insurance card, business cards, copy of marriage license, prepaid phone cards, traveler's checks and receipt (keep receipt in a separate bag), vaccination certificates (if required), a doctor's prescription (for each prescription medication you are bringing)

- A travel Bible; a honeymoon devotional book, such as *Two Hearts Praying as One* (by Dennis Rainey and Barbara Rainey, Multnomah Publishers, 2003); and this book

- Honeymoon journal/notebook and pen(s)

- A novel, magazine or thank-you notes to write (and men, you need to help write these notes)

- Tickets for travel (or a copy of e-ticket confirmations) and tickets (or confirmations) for prebooked events, vouchers/coupons

- Emergency phone numbers and contacts (be sure to take phone numbers for your credit card companies—in case your cards are lost or stolen)

- Moisturizer, sunscreen, lip balm, body lotion

- Travel umbrella and ponchos

- Cell phone(s)

- Camera and film (consider disposable camera and/or a disposable underwater camera—which are *much* more expensive at vacation spots). Don't forget that the newer security scanners can damage some film in your checked or carry-on luggage. Use a special x-ray-proof camera bag for all checked luggage. For carry-on luggage, let the screener know about your film.

- Digital camera, batteries, extra memory, manual

- CD or Mp3 player, batteries, minispeakers

- Foreign-language dictionary or phrase book

- Travel guide(s), guidebooks, maps and directions

- Mini-DVD player or DVD-capable laptop and DVDs

- Reading material(s)

- Beach bag, laundry bag, day pack, fanny pack or money belt

- Electrical adapters/converters (if going outside the United States)

- Contact lens supplies, extra glasses

- Travel clock with alarm

- Earplugs

- Sewing kit

- Instant stain-treatment towelettes

- Large plastic or nylon tote bag for bringing home new purchases

- Eyeglass prescription information (or an extra pair)

- List of food and drug allergies

- Phone numbers (including after-hour emergency phone numbers) for health insurance company and personal physicians

- Copy of your packing list—this one may surprise you, but it will help you while packing up at the end of your trip (to be sure you have everything) and it is worth its weight in gold if any luggage gets lost or stolen.

- Serial numbers of your traveler's checks and 24-hour phone number for reporting loss or theft

- Tourism bureau information numbers

- Special honeymoon gift(s) for your new spouse

- Handheld digital tape recorder (great for recording a memory journal or for bringing along your favorite songs) and/or video camera

PLANNING CALENDAR

More Than Six Months Before the Honeymoon

Travel Planning

❐ Work with your fiancé to write out your honeymoon budget and decide on the length of your trip.

❐ Choose a destination.

❐ Decide on a travel agent.

❐ Consider using a Honeymoon planning service (e.g., Honeymoons by Sunset).

❐ Write a proposed itinerary for your trip.

❐ Begin obtaining or renewing passports and visas if needed.

❐ If traveling internationally, contact travel bureaus and Consulate/Embassy of the country for travel information.

Medical Planning

❐ Calendar out your menstrual cycle for the next several months leading up to your honeymoon, based on your current menstrual schedule.

❐ Call to schedule an appointment with your primary care physician (family physician, gynecologist or internist).

Spiritual Planning

❐ Discuss your beliefs regarding spiritual matters with your fiancé.

❐ Look into the PREPARE and FOCCUS premarital assessments.

❐ Pick one or two books to read together.

❐ Look into financial planning and budgeting training. Dave Ramsey and Crown Ministries both have weekend courses available.

❐ Consider finding a mentor couple you both like and ask them to be your marriage mentors.

❐ Look into Marriage Seminars or weekend conferences that take engaged couples.

Six Months Before the Honeymoon

Travel Planning

❐ Write out itinerary.

❐ Make and confirm travel reservations and send in required deposits.

❐ Use the Internet to investigate honeymoon destinations and details. Compare flight costs at several different sites.

❐ Schedule/arrange flights.

❏ Arrange lodging.
❏ Purchase tickets for special events or theatre seats and/or make dinner reservations.
❏ Reserve rental cars.
❏ Consider registering your honeymoon so that wedding guests can contribute to your honeymoon costs as a wedding gift.
❏ Consider travel insurance or travel protection plans.

Medical Planning
❏ With your fiancé, study the ethical issues surrounding birth control choices.
❏ Check out the Centers for Disease Control and Prevention (CDC) recommendations for immunizations for your travel destination at www.cdc.gov/travel.
❏ Go to your doctor's appointment and make sure to discuss the following:
    ❏ Birth control
    ❏ Prescriptions for travel medications and sleeping medications (if desired)
    ❏ Vaccinations
    ❏ Shift or stopping periods so as not to coincide with the wedding or honeymoon
    ❏ Need for Pap smear and/or sexually transmitted infection testing

Spiritual Planning
❏ Study materials from PREPARE and FOCCUS to decide which premarital inventory is best for you as a couple.
❏ Locate professional or pastoral counselors in your area that use PREPARE or FOCCUS.
❏ Register for premarital counseling together.
❏ Register for a financial planning seminar.
❏ Register for a weekend conference for engaged couples.
❏ If needed, identify Christian counseling resources close to you for working through sexual or emotional baggage issues that you may have identified and begin working to resolve these issues prior to marriage.
❏ Choose a mentor couple and talk to them about meeting with you and your fiancé.
❏ Begin meeting with your marriage mentor couple at least once a month.
❏ Subscribe to Dr. Walt's pre- and postmarriage e-mail encouragements at www.DrWalt.com.
❏ If you are not already attending church or another faith community regularly together, begin searching for one that you will make your spiritual home as a married couple.

Three Months Before the Honeymoon

Travel Planning
❏ Start reviewing and refining the packing list.
❏ Make reservations for pets that may need to be boarded while you are away.
❏ Finalize reservations for honeymoon destinations, restaurants and events and confirm ticket numbers and deposits.

❑ Check with your bank and credit card companies to be sure that your ATM card and credit cards will work at your honeymoon location. Also find out if there are ATM fees there you need to know about.

❑ Request a list of ATMs at your destination from your bank.

❑ Check with your cell phone carrier to see if your cell phone will work where you are traveling.

Medical Planning

❑ Check out travel recommendations for your honeymoon destination at Travel Health Online, www.tripprep.com.

❑ If traveling outside the country, check out travel recommendations for your destination with the CDC at www.cdc.gov/travel.

Spiritual Planning

❑ If possible, begin attending church or another faith community regularly together.

❑ Go through PREPARE or FOCCUS premarital inventory as a couple.

❑ Begin premarital counseling.

❑ Attend a weekend Marriage or Engagement Seminar together.

Two Months Before the Honeymoon

Travel Planning

❑ Make a shopping list and go shopping for your travel needs including:
  ❑ Clothes
  ❑ Lingerie
  ❑ Film/camera
  ❑ Luggage
  ❑ Electrical plug adapters
  ❑ Cellular phone service

❑ Obtain written (e-mail, letter or fax) confirmation numbers for airline tickets, rental car, hotels, etc.

❑ Be sure any final deposits or required payments are made and you get written confirmation of each to carry with you.

❑ Check with your bank to see if your bills and financial obligations can be preprogrammed in advance, online, for automatic payment that will do your bill paying while you are on your trip.

Medical Planning

❑ Finish getting your vaccinations and fill your prescriptions, especially if traveling abroad.

❑ Update any adult vaccines needed (whether you travel or not): e.g., Diphtheria, tetanus, and acellular pertussis (DTaP) booster, chickenpox vaccine (especially for women), influenza vaccine (October to December), etc.

❏ If you are planning to use sleeping medications before your wedding night, while traveling to your honeymoon destination or on your honeymoon, be sure to try them out for several nights to see how they work and to determine if they have any undesirable side effects.

Spiritual Planning

❏ If you can find a small-group Bible study or Sunday School class with young marrieds that you'd like to attend, ask the group about starting to attend now. This can be a powerful support group for you as you prepare for marriage

❏ If you have not already, ask a small group of friends and family to begin to pray for you individually and as a couple for the rest of your engagement and during the first year of your marriage.

❏ You may wish to consider e-mailing a list of prayer requests to these folks once a week—or even once a day as the wedding gets closer. Or, ask your mentor couple or a close friend to do this for you.

One Month Before the Honeymoon

Travel Planning

❏ Make sure your homeowner's insurance covers the items inside your house, including new wedding gifts, in your absence—and if travel insurance is available.

❏ Check to see if your car insurance will cover your rental car and both drivers at your honeymoon location.

❏ Identify a house-sitter to look in on your house during your trip.

❏ Be sure you have all the luggage you need for the trip.

❏ Shop for any camera or electronic needs you'll have on your trip.

❏ Photocopy your itinerary and all travel documents. Have at least one copy to leave at home and at least one copy to carry with you.

Medical Planning

❏ Go back to the Travel Health Online (www.tripprep.com) and CDC (www.cdc.gov/travel) websites and write down the names of the medical resources where you will be traveling, in case you need medical care on your trip.

Spiritual Planning

❏ If you have not already, ask your pastoral professional, mentor couple and family to begin praying daily for you.

❏ If you have not already, begin praying together, as a couple, every day.

❏ Consider reading one of these "sex" books (yep, even if you're sexually experienced!):
  • Dr. William Cutrer's book *Sexual Intimacy in Marriage* (especially chapter 6)
  • Dr. Louis McBurney's book *Real Questions: Real Answers About Sex* (especially chapter 3)
  • Dr. Ed Wheat's book *Intended for Pleasure*

Two Weeks Before the Honeymoon

Travel Planning

❏ Get your marriage license! Some states require up to 72 hours wait between the time the license is applied for and when it can be obtained. Others require a wait of up to 3 days after obtaining the license before you can be legally married! To find out what your state requirements are, go to your County Clerk's office.

❏ Pick up tickets (if paper tickets are required) from your travel agent and check all numbers and personal information.

❏ Purchase traveler's checks and get your travel cash.

❏ Be sure your camera battery is fully charged (and chargeable). Purchase extra film, batteries or memory.

❏ Go over your packing list one last time and get anything else you need.

❏ Assemble tickets, boarding passes and all important documents.

❏ Have any clothes altered, laundered or dry-cleaned.

❏ Begin setting out things to pack.

Medical Planning

❏ Get your blood drawn, if your state requires it for marriage. For a full list of states, go to http://www.nolo.com/article.cfm/ObjectID/586AC0B4-0435-4D7C -BD06608979A6CBF9/catID/697DBAFE-20FF-467A-9E9395985EE7E825/118/ 304/192/ART/

❏ Create your Honeymoon Kit.

❏ Check with the TSA, your airline or your travel agent to see what restrictions apply to your carry-on luggage and carry-on Honeymoon Kit.

Spiritual Planning

❏ Visit one last time with your spiritual support team—premarital counselor, pastor, mentor couple, small group. Ask them to pray for you during these last two weeks and during your honeymoon.

One Week Before the Honeymoon

Travel Planning

❏ Start packing. Be sure everything will fit in the bags. Do *not* wait until your wedding night!

❏ If you're considering sending your luggage ahead, call to make or reconfirm arrangements.

❏ Call your credit card companies and let them know where you will be traveling.

❏ Schedule stops for mail and newspaper delivery while away.

❏ Check out the current traveling conditions and weather conditions of your travel destination at Travel Health Online or weather.com.

- ❑ Arrange for a friend or family member to pick up registered gifts, or place them on hold in your absence.
- ❑ If necessary, arrange for a friend to pick up your wedding clothes and return the groom's tux, if rented.
- ❑ Deliver the photocopies of your itinerary and travel documents to your house-sitter or family.
- ❑ Confirm all travel reservations and all tickets.
- ❑ Make and pack a list of addresses and stationery for thank-you notes.
- ❑ Arrange transportation from the wedding to the airport or the location of your wedding night.

Medical Planning
- ❑ Fill your prescriptions and pack them in your Honeymoon Kit.
- ❑ Pack your Honeymoon Kit in your carry-on bag, to be kept with you at all times, just in case your checked luggage gets lost or delayed.
- ❑ Be sure to check one last time on what the airline prohibits from your carry-on bag.

Spiritual Planning
- ❑ Read the chapters in this book specific to you as the bride or the groom.
- ❑ Consider reading together, as a couple, any parts of the "sex" book that you've been reading that have been particularly meaningful to you.
- ❑ Write a romantic love letter to your spouse-to-be to read to him or her on your honeymoon, if you have not yet done so.

One to Two Days Before the Honeymoon

- ❑ Put this book, with all your tickets and travel papers in your carry-on.
- ❑ Make sure your Honeymoon Kit is in your carry-on and complies with all TSA travel regulations for carry-ons.
- ❑ Clean out the refrigerator. Empty the garbage. Set light timers. Mow the lawn or arrange to have it mowed. Buy flight items, such as magazines, books, gum, etc.
- ❑ Set up automatic reply on your e-mail and change the message on your voice mail.
- ❑ Check the weather for your destination one last time.
- ❑ Double-check to be sure you have all your travel documents, driver's license, marriage license or certificate, passport and visa, currency, traveler's checks, electronics, etc.
- ❑ Call your airline one last time to confirm your flight. Ask if a notification service that will let you know of any last-minute changes is available (many airlines will call your cell phone or e-mail you).
- ❑ Pack some nonperishable food in your carry-on luggage (crackers, granola bars, water, etc.). Stay current with regulations for what you can bring on the airplane.
- ❑ Arrange for someone to bring your luggage to the reception and someone to pack you each a doggie bag of food from the reception if you plan on leaving directly from the reception to your hotel.

❏ Take a moment from your busy day to reflect on your last day as a single person. Pray for your marriage, your soon-to-be spouse and your future family. Thank God for all the wonderful blessings in your life and His love for you and your fiancé.

❏ Get a good night's sleep, with the contentment that comes with knowing that whatever challenges arise tomorrow, by the end of the day, you will be joined as husband and wife—in the marriage of a lifetime and the marriage for a lifetime. And that's what matters most. All the rest is minor detail.

MEDICAL DOCUMENTS AND INFORMATION

The purpose of this section is to provide a place to gather all pertinent medical information in preparation for the honeymoon.

Medical Documents Checklist

❐ Copy of your insurance cards, stored in a different place from your originals. You might consider putting the copy in a pocket folder, which will be packed in your carry-on bag. Your original insurance cards and identification information could be stored either on your person or in your wallet or purse.

❐ Prescriptions—to be filled a week or two before you leave (list)

Hers   *His*

_____   _____
_____   _____
_____   _____
_____   _____

❐ Your physicians' names and office phone numbers in case you need to contact them while you are away

His: Dr._____Phone Number:_____
Hers: Dr._____Phone Number:_____

❐ Closest medical facility to each destination on your itinerary. Again, simpler is better. Look up online at Travel Health Online, www.tripprep.com.

Clinic Name:_____
Address:_____
_____
Phone Number:_____

Clinic Name:_____
Address:_____
_____
Phone Number:_____

Clinic Name:_____

Address:_____

_____

Phone Number:_____

Clinic Name:_____

Address:_____

_____

Phone Number:_____

Medical Documentation and Information Form

	Bride's Medical Information	*Groom's Medical Information*
Full Name (including maiden)		
Date of Birth		
Insurance Carrier		
Insurance Numbers		
Insurance Company Phone #		
Social Security Number		
Emergency Contact Name and Phone Number		
Medical Conditions and Medical Alerts		
Medical Allergies		
Current Medications— name, dosage, and timing of administration		
Name and Dates of Vaccinations		

Appendix E

MENSTRUAL
CALENDARS

I t's a good idea to start keeping track of your menstrual cycles, even if you've never done it before. Keeping a menstrual calendar can help you predict your fertility and your next period, and it can alert you to irregularities in your cycle that may indicate a medical problem. You should bring your menstrual calendar with you to all of your medical appointments. Your doctor will be so impressed!

Use the first calendar on this page to chart out your last 3 to 6 cycles. Count the number of days from the first day of bleeding of one cycle to the first day of bleeding for the next one. That is your cycle length. Take the average of 3 cycles to determine your average cycle length. Using this information, chart into the future to predict when your period will fall around the dates of your wedding and honeymoon. Feel free to make copies of these blank calendar pages for your personal use.

Instructions: Mark the days of your bleeding in the boxes corresponding to the date.

- • = spotting
- ✓ = regular day
- ✗ = heavy day

Year___	1	2	3	4	5	6	7	8	9	10	11	12	13	14	15	16	17	18	19	20	21	22	23	24	25	26	27	28	29	30	31
January																															
February																															
March																															
April																															
May																															
June																															
July																															
August																															
September																															
October																															
November																															
December																															

Year___	1	2	3	4	5	6	7	8	9	10	11	12	13	14	15	16	17	18	19	20	21	22	23	24	25	26	27	28	29	30	31
January																															
February																															
March																															
April																															
May																															
June																															
July																															
August																															
September																															
October																															
November																															
December																															

Year____	1	2	3	4	5	6	7	8	9	10	11	12	13	14	15	16	17	18	19	20	21	22	23	24	25	26	27	28	29	30	31
January																															
February																															
March																															
April																															
May																															
June																															
July																															
August																															
September																															
October																															
November																															
December																															

TRAVEL DOCUMENTS
AND INFORMATION

The purpose of this section is to provide a place to gather all pertinent travel information in preparation for the honeymoon.

Travel Agent Information

Name of Agency:_____

Name of Agent:_____

Address:_____

Phone Numbers:_____

Responsible for reservations for the following (list):

- Airline Reservations_____

- Hotels_____

- Rental Car_____

- Taxi or Limo_____

- Dinner Reservations_____

- Special Events or Vouchers

  - _____

  - _____

  - _____

  - _____

  - _____

- Appointment for pick-up of all tickets and vouchers
  (2 weeks prior to wedding—date and time)_____

- Confirm all information on tickets and vouchers is correct

- Payment arrangements:

  _____

  _____

  _____

Notes:_____

_____

_____

Travel Documents Checklist

Copy of Social Security cards	His ☐	Hers ☐
Copy of driver's licenses	His ☐	Hers ☐
Passports (if traveling out of country)	His ☐	Hers ☐
Visas (if necessary)	His ☐	Hers ☐
Copy of marriage license	His ☐	Hers ☐
Airline tickets, for all legs of journey	His ☐	Hers ☐

(Make all of your bride's reservations in her maiden name, unless you will have time to change her name on all identification, or you plan on showing your marriage license along the way.)

Vouchers for events	His ☐	Hers ☐
Hotel reservations	His and Hers	☐
Traveler's checks	His ☐	Hers ☐
Check numbers:		
_____	His ☐	Hers ☐
_____	His ☐	Hers ☐

Itinerary Overview
Use this table as an overview for planning your honeymoon, using the subsequent daily planning pages for writing in confirmation numbers, contacts, phone numbers and other details.

	Travel	Lodging	Special Events and Dining	Budget
Wedding Night Date_____				$
Day 1 Date_____				$
Day 2 Date_____				$
Day 3 Date_____				$
Day 4 Date_____				$
Day 5 Date_____				$
Day 6 Date_____				$
Day 7 Date_____				$
Total honeymoon budget				$

Honeymoon Daily Travel Planning Pages
Wedding Night (or first few days if staying at your new apartment/home)

Date(s):_____ Budget: $_____

Travel from reception to lodging:_____

Name of company (and driver, if using one):_____

_____

Phone number and contact name:_____

Time and location to pick up:_____

Payment arrangements:_____

Reservation confirmation number:_____

Date of confirmation (week before):_____

Lodging:_____

Place:_____

Address:_____

Phone number and contact name:_____

Date/time of arrival and departure:_____

Special instructions:_____

Payment arrangements:_____

Reservation confirmation number:_____

Date confirmed (week before):_____

Reminders

What and when are you going to eat? It's helpful for you to have someone pack you both a doggie bag from the reception to take with you to your hotel. Many a bride and groom have spent the whole reception shaking hands, dancing and cutting cake, only to find at the end that they've forgotten to eat!

Name:_____

How are you getting your luggage to the hotel? The traditional birdseed- or rice-throwing scene leaving the reception leaves little room for you each to be lugging suitcases! Make sure you have assigned one of your attendants to get your bags from your house or the reception into your car or to the hotel.

Name:_____

*Honeymoon Day 1 Destination*_____

Date:_____

Transportation from lodging to airport:_____

Name of company (and driver, if using one):_____

_____

Phone number and contact name:_____

Time and location to pick up:_____

Payment arrangements:_____

Reservation confirmation number:_____

Date of confirmation (week before):_____

Airline Reservations:_____

Airport and airline:_____

Departure info (include flight number, seats, time and date of departure):_____

Arriving at _____ (city/airport)

at _____ (time/date)

Departure info (include flight number, seats, time and date of departure):_____

Arriving at _____ (city/airport)

at _____ (time/date)

Departure info (include flight number, seats, time and date of departure):_____

Arriving at _____ (city/airport)

at _____ (time/date)

Departure info (include flight number, seats, time and date of departure):_____

Arriving at _____ (city/airport)

at _____ (time/date)

Payment arrangements:_____

Reservation confirmation number:_____

Date confirmed (week before):_____

Transportation from airport to lodging:_____

Name of company (and driver, if using one):_____

_____

Phone number and contact name:_____

Time and location to pick up:_____

Payment arrangements:_____

Reservation confirmation number:_____

Date of confirmation (week before):_____

Lodging:_____

    Place:_____

    Address:_____

    Phone number and contact name:_____

    Date/time of arrival and departure:_____

    Special instructions:_____

    Payment arrangements:_____

    Reservation confirmation number:_____

    Date confirmed (week before):_____

Reminder:

Time change?—If you'll be crossing time lines, especially many of them, you may want to remember to set your watch to remember to take time-sensitive prescriptions such as birth control.

    Time difference between destination and home—lose/gain ___ hours

ACKNOWLEDGMENTS
AND AUTHORS' NOTES

First of all, we are both eternally grateful to our Creator, whose divine design for love, courtship, the honeymoon and marriage has eternally changed our lives. We're also grateful to our faith communities who have taught and mentored each of us in our marriages.

We are both indebted to our soul mates and spouses, Barb Larimore and Dale Crockett, for their careful review of the manuscript and many wonderful suggestions to improve it. We are also indebted to our patients who have helped us develop this information and these recommendations over many years. Without their input and feedback, this book would not have been written.

I am appreciative of the individuals who helped me with the "For the Groom's Eyes Only" chapter. Thanks to Rev. Andy Braner; Dwight Bain; Rev. J. B. Collingsworth; Ed Dawson, MS; Harvey Elder, MD; Mark Elfstrand; Reg Finger, MD; John Fuller; David Hager, MD; Warren Heffron, MD; Rev. Gus Kinchen; Tom Mason; Byron Paulus; Wayne Pederson; Boone and Peggy Powell; Morgan Snyder; and Dennis Swanberg, PhD. A special thank-you is also due to Mike and Harriet McManus, the founders of Marriage Savers, as well as Dr. Louis and Melissa McBurney, for their assistance.

I'm grateful to my son, Scott Bonham Larimore, and his wife-for-life of one year, Jennifer Lynn Larimore (soon to be Jennifer Larimore, PhD), for allowing me to share their stories and experiences with you.

We're grateful to those who took the time to review the manuscript to assist us in being sure that the advice you are reading is biblically sound: Interim Pastor Steve Hixon and the Elder Board (Chairman Doug Jenkins, Jeff Ball, Rick Fisher, Dave Flower, Ron Rathburn and Eric Swierczek) from Walt's home church, Little Log Church in Palmer Lake,

Colorado; Pastor Robert Emmitt and the Elder Board from Sue's home church, Community Bible Church, in San Antonio, Texas; Rev. Andy Braner; David Crockett, PhD; Rev. and Mrs. Robert Emmitt; Rev. Gus Kinchen; Rev. Layne Lebo; Kaitlyn MacMillan; and Morgan Snyder.

We're also so very grateful to those health professionals who took so much of their valuable time to review the manuscript to be sure that the advice we are offering is medically reliable and evidence-based: Adrian Blackwell; Fred Brown, MD; David Crockett, PhD; William Cutrer, MD; Ed Dawson, MS; Caroline Hedges, MD; Donna J. Harrison, MD; Jeremy Hedges, MD; Burritt Hess, MD; Mindy Hess, RN; Leanna Hollis, MD; Julian Hsu, MD; Beth Jewell, MD; Michael McManus, PhD; Dean Patton, MD; Jorge Peacher, MD; and Kent Shih, MD.

Thanks to Lee Hough at Alive Communications for shepherding this project from its conception until its birth. Thanks, Lee, for the coaching and counsel—mixed with your friendship and fellowship. This book would likely not have been printed without your skill and expertise. Also, our appreciation to Ned McLeod, Esq., who provided legal expertise and excellent counsel, not to mention his warmhearted friendship.

We are so very grateful to my many (anonymous) women friends and members of the SSBoard who participated in our Honeymoon Survey. Without their courage and willingness to pass on the wisdom from their own honeymoon experiences and marriages, this book would have been much less helpful.

Sue expresses her gratitude to the following women for their personal help with the manuscript: Barbara Crockett, Sharron Gonzalez, Maria Hey, Ginger Lambert, Stephanie Lisciandro, Jennifer McCarville, Lori Crowley, Ann Olsta, Kristine Olsta, Andrea Pocreva, and Ronda Silliman. And Sue offers this special thank-you to the Elder Board from Community Bible Church, in San Antonio, Texas, and Pastor Robert Emmitt (whose words of wisdom from the pulpit have so permeated her brain on these topics that at times it is impossible for her to separate her thoughts from those planted by the resonance of his voice). Additional thanks to Julie Emmitt and Heather Emmitt Rogers for their very personal contributions and encouragement for the writing of this book.

Last, but not least, our heartfelt thanks go to Alex Field and the entire team at Regal Books for their vision and labor in bringing this resource to you, our readers. We are also appreciative of their professional and prudent editing suggestions and skills that kept many errors from appearing in these pages. However, for any remaining mistakes, I take full credit.

Walt Larimore, MD
Monument, Colorado
October 2006

ENDNOTES

Chapter 2: The Divine Design for Marriage

1. R. David Freedman, "Woman Power Equal to Man," *Biblical Archeology Review,* Jan/Feb 1983. The article can be viewed at http://home.uchicago.edu/~spackman/powerequaltoman.pdf (accessed October 25, 2006). Freeman adds, "Remember that Proverbs 31:10 describes the perfect wife as . . . 'the woman of strength,' which corresponds to the masculine . . . 'the man of strength' (Genesis 47:6, etc.)."
2. David Mills, "The Marital Dance," *Touchstone,* vol. 18, no. 8 (Oct. 2005), p. 3. Used with permission.

Chapter 3: Invest in Stay-Married Insurance!

1. "Divorce Rates." *Americans for Divorce Reform.* http://www.divorcereform.org/rates.html (accessed September 9, 2006).
2. The Bible and Basic Causes of Divorce, *The Interactive Bible.* http://www.bible.ca/f-8causes-divorce .htm (accessed September 9, 2006).
3. The PREPARE/ENRICH Inventory has a somewhat secular perspective. Via 195 statements, the inventory targets marriage expectations, personality issues, communication issues, conflict resolution, finances, having fun together, sexual issues, parenting, dealing with family and friends, spirituality and flexibility. I recommend that whenever possible you and your fiancé do these sessions together with a counselor and *not* in a class situation.

    Here's a website with frequently asked questions (FAQs) about PREPARE: http://marriage .about.com/gi/dynamic/offsite.htm?zi=1/XJ&sdn=marriage&zu=http%3A%2F%2Fwww. lifeinnovations.com%2Foverview%2Ffaq.html.

    If you can't find a premarital counselor in your area, call Focus on the Family, toll-free, at 1-800-A-FAMILY for names of competent Christian counselors in your area. Then you can consult one or more to see who uses the PREPARE materials. Or you can visit the website of Life Innovations (www.lifeinnovations.org) and seek the names of clergy or counselors who administer PREPARE by state.

    You can also seek a premarital counselor in your area via this website: http://marriage .about.com/gi/dynamic/offsite.htm?zi=1/XJ&sdn=marriage&zu=http%3A%2F%2Fwww. lifeinnovations.com%2Foverview%2Ffaq.html
4. FOCCUS is a 156-item instrument (with an additional 33 optional items for interfaith couples, cohabiting couples and couples in which one or both partners are remarrying) that was developed in 1984 through 1986, updated with cohabiting couple items in 1997 and revised in 2000 with new research-based items in the areas related to spirituality and religion. You can learn more about the FOCCUS Inventory at http://www.foccusinc.com/ or http://www.foccusinc.com/sections/foccus_content.asp?PKID=11.
5. Catherine Latimer and Michael J. McManus, "How to Give Marriage Insurance to Premarital Couples," December 30, 2003. http://marriagesavers.org/Marriage%20Insurance.htm (accessed September 9, 2006).
6. Ibid.
7. RELATE is a clinically validated assessment that helps you understand how factors in your family life, personality and values, social interactions and relationships will affect your later marital quality. The assessment includes more than 200 questions, after which you receive a detailed report to help you interpret your (and your fiancé's) responses. You can learn more at www.relate-institute.org.
8. Scott Larimore, personal e-mail communication, March 7, 2006. Used with permission.

9.   Paul Meier, MD, personal e-mail communication, September 12, 2006. Used with permission.
10. Ibid.
11. Jennifer Larimore, personal e-mail communication, March 7, 2006. Used with permission.
12. I also recommend couples strongly consider a Crown Ministry course for learning biblical financial concepts. You can learn more about Crown Financial Ministry at http://www.crown.org/.

   One option is to find and attend a weekend seminar, like their Journey to Financial Freedom Seminar. You can learn more about this seminar and seminar locations at http://www.crown.org/FinancialWisdom/church/jtff.asp. An even better option is to find a church offering Crown Ministry training for couples. You can find a local contact to call in your area at this website: http://secure.crown.org/content/ourlocations/default.asp.

   Financial Peace: Restoring Financial Hope to You and Your Family by Dave Ramsey is an excellent book. The newer version of this book is titled *Financial Peace: Revisited*. In some areas, you can find a Dave Ramsey course at local churches. These courses are excellent.
13. Consider attending an Engaged Encounter Weekend. You can learn more about Engaged Encounter and find a contact near you at http://www.angelfire.com/in/ummelaf/whatee.html, or you can call 303-753-9407 (Protestant) or 714-821-8680 (Catholic).

   Another option is to attend a Weekend to Remember. These weekend courses are primarily attended by married couples, but engaged couples are welcome and there are special sessions for engaged couples. You can learn more at http://www.familylife.com/conferences/marriage.asp or call 1-800-FL-TODAY (1-800-358-6329) OR 1-877-FL-TODAY (Español).
14. To find out if there are trained Marriage Savers couples in your area, call 301-469-5873 or send an e-mail to Mike@MarriageSavers.org. Or you could check with your pastor to see if he or she has a couple he or she would recommend for you.
15. Latimer and McManus, "How to Give Marriage Insurance to Premarital Couples."
16. Ibid.
17. Ibid.
18. Jennifer Larimore, personal e-mail communication, March 7, 2006. Used with permission.
19. Michael J. McManus, personal e-mail communications, December 20-27, 2005. Used with permission.
20. Paul James Birch, Stan E. Weed and Joseph A. Olsen, "Assessing the Impact of Community Marriage Policies on U.S. County Divorce Rates. Executive Summary," *The Institute for Research and Evaluation,* March 2004. http://www.smartmarriages.com/cmp.weed.pdf (accessed September 9, 2006).
21. *Marriage Savers.* www.marriagesavers.org/ (accessed September 9, 2006).
22. *Right Start Publications LLC.* www.rightstartpublications.com/ (accessed September 9, 2006).
23. For more information, call Marriage Savers at 301-469-5873 or send an e-mail to Mike@MarriageSavers.org.
24. The Bible and Basic Causes of Divorce, *The Interactive Bible.* http://www.bible.ca/f-8causes-divorce.htm (accessed September 9, 2006).

Chapter 4: Safe Sex? Save Sex!
1.   "Safe Sex," *About.* http://marriage.about.com/cs/sex/g/safesex.htm (accessed September 9, 2006).
2.   "Safe Sex," Medical Encyclopedia, *Medline Plus.* http://www.nlm.nih.gov/medlineplus/ency/article/001949.htm (accessed September 9, 2006).
3.   "Safe Sex," *Wikipedia.* http://en.wikipedia.org/wiki/Safe_sex (accessed October 25, 2006).
4.   "Frequently Asked Questions: How Effective Are Condoms in Preventing STIs?" *The Medical Institute for Sexual Health.* http://www.medinstitute.org/health/questions_answers.html#listitem1766-7467 (accessed September 9, 2006).
5.   "Condoms and STDs," *The Medical Institute for Sexual Health.* http://www.medinstitute.org/includes/downloads/condomsstds.pdf (accessed September 9, 2006).
6.   Edward O. Laumann, John H. Gagnon, Robert T. Michael, and Stuart Michaels, *The Social Organization of Sexuality—Sexual Practices in the United States—The Complete Findings from America's Most Comprehensive Survey of Sexual Behavior* (Chicago, IL: University of Chicago Press, 1994), pp. 86–93.

7.   Ibid.
8.   Ibid.
9.   David Gudgel, *Before You Live Together* (Ventura, CA: Regal Books, 2003).
10. David Gudgel, "Why You Shouldn't Live Together (Part 2 of 2)," *family.org*. http://www.family.org/ fmedia/broadcast/a0039130.cfm?&refcd=OL06XRDRC&tvar=n (accessed September 9, 2006).
11. Craig Glickman, *Solomon's Song of Love* (West Monroe, LA: Howard Books, 2003).
12. You can learn more about Bsafe Online at http://www.bsafehome.com/.

Chapter 5: From Past Sex to Perfect Love

1.   "Yoda Quotes," *ThinkExist.com.* http://en.thinkexist.com/quotation/fear_is_the_path_to _the_dark_side-fear_leads_to/255552.html (accessed September 9, 2006).
2.   Donald Grey Barnhouse, quoted in Gladys Hunt, *A Persuaded Heart: A Woman's Potential for Genuine Freedom* (Grand Rapids, MI: Discovery House Publishers, 1991), n.p.
3.   Michael J. McManus, personal e-mail communications, December 20-27, 2006. Used with permission.
4.   Ibid.
5.   Ibid.
6.   Ibid.
7.   Walt Larimore, *God's Design for the Highly Healthy Person* (Grand Rapids, MI: Zondervan Publishing House, 2004). Available at www.DrWalt.com/books/.
8.   Ibid., pp. 91-109.

Chapter 6: A Healthy Honeymoon

1.   Constitution of the World Health Organization, Geneva, Switzerland, 1948. http://www.searo .who.int/EN/Section898/Section1441.htm (accessed October 25, 2006).
2.   D. Dean Patton, MD, personal e-mail communication, January 10, 2001. Quoted in Walt Larimore, *God's Design for the Highly Healthy Person* (Grand Rapids, MI: Zondervan Publishing House, 2004), p. 28.
3.   John Wilkinson. *The Bible and Healing: A Medical and Theological Commentary* (Grand Rapids, MI: W.B. Eerdmans, 2000), p. 7.
4.   Walt Larimore, *God's Design for the Highly Healthy Person* (Grand Rapids, MI: Zondervan Publishing House, 2004). Available at www.DrWalt.com/books/.
5.   "Chart: State Marriage License and Blood Test Requirements," *Nolo.* http://www.nolo.com/ article.cfm/ObjectID/586AC0B4-0435-4D7C-BD06608979A6CBF9/catID/697DBAFE -20FF-467A-9E9395985EE7E825/118/304/192/ART/ (accessed September 10, 2006).
6.   "Men's Health," *Doctors 4 U.* http://www.doctors-4u.com/mens_health.htm (accessed September 10, 2006).
7.   Larimore. *God's Design for the Highly Healthy Person.*
8.   Both Sue and I have published a number of reference articles on this topic:
     (a)   Walter L. Larimore, "Postfertilization Effects of Oral Contraceptives and Their Relationship to Informed Consent," *Archives of Family Medicine,* vol. 9 (2000), pp. 126-133. The article can be viewed online at http://www.polycarp.org/larimore_stanford.htm (accessed October 25, 2006).
     (b)   Walt Larimore and Randy Alcorn, "Using the Birth Control Pill Is Ethically Unacceptable," quoted in J. F. Kilner, P. C. Paige and W. D. Hager, eds., *The Reproduction Revolution: A Christian Appraisal of Sexuality, Reproductive Technologies and the Family* (Grand Rapids, MI: William B. Eerdmans, 2000), pp. 179-191.
     (c)   Walter L. Larimore, "The Abortifacient Effect of the Birth Control Pill and the Principle of 'Double Effect,'" *Ethics and Medicine,* vol. 16, no. 1 (2000), pp. 23-30. The article can be viewed online at http://www.epm.org/pilldebate2.html (accessed October 25, 2006).
     (d)   Susan A. Crockett, Joseph DeCook, Donna Harrison and C. Hersh, "Hormone Contraceptives Controversies and Clarifications," *ProLife Obstetrician,* April 1999.

    (e)   Susan A. Crockett, Joseph DeCook, Donna Harrison and C. Hersh, "Using Hormone Contraceptives Is a Decision Involving Science, Scripture and Conscience," quoted in J. F. Kilner, P. C. Paige and W. D. Hager, eds., *The Reproduction Revolution: A Christian Appraisal of Sexuality, Reproductive Technologies, and the Family* pp. 192–201.

9.   See William Cutrer and Sandra Glahn, *The Contraception Guidebook: Options, Risks, and Answers for Christian Couples* (Grand Rapids, MI: Zondervan Publishing House, 2005). Here are some views you can study:

    (a)   "Possible Post-fertilization Effects of Hormonal Birth Control," Christian Medical and Dental Associations. This position statement can be viewed at http://www.cmawashington.org/index.cgi?BISKIT=7049854&CONTEXT=art&art=1183 (accessed October 25, 2006).

    (b)   "Birth Control Pills and Other Hormonal Contraception," Focus on the Family Position Statement. This position statement can be viewed at http://family.org/corrpdfs/Miscellaneous/Position_Statement-Birth_Control_Pills_and_Other_Hormonal_Contraception.pdf (3).

    (c)   Randy Alcorn, *A Dialogue About Birth Control* (Sandy, OR: Eternal Perspective Ministries, 1999). Available at http://www.epm.org/articles/dialogue.html (accessed October 25, 2006)

    (d)   Randy Alcorn, *Does the Birth Control Pill Cause Abortions?* 5th ed. (Sandy, OR: Eternal Perspective Ministries, 2000). Available at http://www.epm.org/bcp.html (accessed October 25, 2006).

    (e)   Robert Fleischmann, *The Christian and Birth Control: the Pill* (Milwaukee, WI: Wisconsin Evangelical Lutheran Synod Lutherans for Life, 1999). You can search their website, from their home page, http://www.wels.net/, for several articles on birth control and the birth control pill. You can find several examples on these sites:

        http://www.wels.net/cgi-bin/site.pl?1518&cuItem_itemID=497&cuTopic_topicID=27

        http://www.wels.net/cgi-bin/site.pl?1518&cuItem_itemID=6145&cuTopic_topicID=22

        http://www.wels.net/cgi-bin/site.pl?1518&cuItem_itemID=6141&cuTopic_topicID=27

        http://www.wels.net/cgi-bin/site.pl?1518&cuItem_itemID=6243&cuTopic_topicID=26

    (f)   William F. Colliton, Jr., "Is It an Abortifacient and Contraceptive? Believe It—the Answer Is Yes!" Available at http://www.all.org/article.php?id=10193 (accessed October 25, 2006).

    (g)   Trewhella, M. "The Protest of a Protestant Minister Against Birth Control." *Missionaries to the Preborn.* http://www.missionariestopreborn.com/default.asp?fuseaction=bc_protestantprotest (accessed September 10, 2006).

10.   "Recommended Adult Immunization Schedule, by Vaccine and Age Group, October 2005–September 2006," *Centers for Disease Control and Prevention.* http://www.cdc.gov/nip/recs/adult-schedule.pdf (accessed September 10, 2006).

Chapter 7: Honeymoon Travel Concerns

1.   Michael Medved, quoted in Tom Nevin, "Banish the Honeymoon," *Focus on the Family with Dr. James Dobson,* 2000. Available at http://www.family.org/fofmag/marriage/a0010566.cfm (accessed November 6, 2005).

2.   Ibid.

3.   Ibid.

4.   Ibid.

5.   Ibid.

Chapter 8: For the Bride's Eyes Only
1.   Unlike the preceding chapters, which were written from Walt's voice, this chapter is written from Sue to you as the bride-to-be, woman to woman.
2.   *Merriam-Webster Online,* s.v. "intercourse." http://www.m-w.com/dictionary/intercourse (accessed September 11, 2006).
3.   "Sex During Menstruation," *A True Church.* http://www.atruechurch.info/sexduringmenstruation .html (accessed September 11, 2006).
         David Miller, "Homosexuality and Female Menses," *Apologetics Press.org.* http://www .apologeticspress.org/articles/2645 (accessed September 11, 2006).

Chapter 9: For the Groom's Eyes Only
1.   Louis McBurney and Melissa McBurney, *Real Questions, Real Answers About Sex* (Grand Rapids, MI: Zondervan Publishing House, 2006), pp. 45–47.
2.   Morgan Snyder, personal e-mail communication, March 6, 2006. Used with permission.
3.   *Merriam-Webster Online,* s.v. "intercourse." http://www.m-w.com/dictionary/intercourse (accessed September 11, 2006).
4.   "The Husbands Speak: Words of Advice from Great Guys Who've Been Altared," *About.* http://honeymoons.about.com/cs/sex/a/husbandspeak.htm (accessed September 11, 2006).
5.   David Hager, personal e-mail communication, December 20, 2005. Used with permission.
6.   McBurney and McBurney, *Real Questions, Real Answers About Sex,* p. 56.

Conclusion
1.   Lyle Dorsett, personal e-mail communication, March 7, 2006.

SCRIPTURE INDEX

SUBJECT INDEX

Other Resources by Walt Larimore, MD

Bryson City Tales:
Stories of a Doctor's First Year of Practice in the Smoky Mountains

Bryson City Seasons:
More Tales of a Doctor's Practice in the Smoky Mountains

Bryson City Secrets:
Even More Tales of a Small-Town Doctor in the Smoky Mountains

Best of Bryson City audio

Alternative Medicine:
The Christian Handbook
(coauthored with Dónal O'Mathúna)

God's Design for the Highly Healthy Person
(with Traci Mullins)

God's Design for the Highly Healthy Child
(with Stephen and Amanda Sorenson)

God's Design for the Highly Healthy Teen
(with Mike Yorkey)

Going Public with Your Faith:
Becoming a Spiritual Influence at Work
(coauthored with William Carr Peel)

Going Public with Your Faith:
Becoming a Spiritual Influence at Work audio
(coauthored with William Carr Peel)

Going Public with Your Faith:
Becoming a Spiritual Influence at Work—Groupware™ curriculum
with video, DVD, leader's guide and participant's workbook
(coauthored with William Carr Peel, with Stephen and Amanda
Sorenson)

Lintball Leo's Not-So-Stupid Questions About Your Body
(with John Riddle, illustrated by Mike Phillips)

Why ADHD Doesn't Mean Disaster
(coauthored with Dennis Swanberg and Diane Passno)

Ten Essentials of Highly Healthy People
(with Traci Mullins)

The Highly Healthy Child
(with Stephen and Amanda Sorenson)

The Saline Solution:
Becoming a Spiritual Influence in Your Medical Practice
small-group curriculum with video, leader's guide and participant's
workbook (coauthored with William Carr Peel)

SuperSized Kids:
How to Rescue Your Child from the Obesity Threat
(coauthored with Cheryl Flynt and Steve Halliday)

More Books That Offer
Big Help for Relationships